The Buddhism of Tibet

THE WISDOM OF TIBET SERIES

The Buddhism of Tibet
 H.H. the Dalai Lama

Tantra in Tibet
 H.H. the Dalai Lama
 Tsong-ka-pa
 Jeffrey Hopkins

Deity Yoga
 H.H. the Dalai Lama
 Tsong-ka-pa
 Jeffrey Hopkins

The Buddhism of Tibet

His Holiness the Dalai Lama

Translated and Edited by Jeffrey Hopkins

Snow Lion Publications
Ithaca, New York USA

Snow Lion Publications
P.O. Box 6483
Ithaca, New York 14851
USA

Printed in USA

ISBN 0-937938-48-3

Library of Congress Cataloging-in-Publication Data

The Buddhism of Tibet.

Includes index.
Contents: The Buddhism of Tibet / by The Dalai
Lama — The key to the Middle Way / by The Dalai
Lama — The precious Garland / by Nagarjuna —
The song of the four mindfulnesses / by the 7th Dalai
Lama.
1. Buddhism—China—Tibet—Doctrines—Collected
works. 2. Mādhyamika (Buddhism)—Collected works.
I. Bstan-'dzin-rgya-mtsho, Dalai Lama XIV, 1935-
II. Nāgārjuna, 2nd cent. III. Bskal-bzan-rgya-mtsho,
Dalai Lama VII, 1708-1757.
BQ7634.B83   1987   294.3'923   87-13049
ISBN 0-937938-48-3

*Published under the aegis of
the Library of Tibetan Works and Archives
with the authority of
His Holiness the Dalai Lama
as revealing oral tradition*

Foreword

Sentient beings in general and mankind in particular have made and are continuing to make efforts to bring about their happiness and comfort by many different methods in accordance with their varying abilities. However, through a multitude of bad causes, both external and internal, they are continually tormented by many sufferings such as mental agitation and so forth. People in particular, unlike other living beings, create disturbances for themselves and others by reason of differences such as of country, race, political system and theory. As a result of these differences, groups of men are amassed, war is made and so on. Like intentionally putting a finger in its own eye, mankind consciously engages in many techniques that bring various undesirable consequences upon itself, such as causes for fear, man-made diseases, starvation and untimely death.

I have thought that under the circumstances of such a delicate time as described above, it would be wonderful if even a few people for a short period could have some internal peace. Also, many intelligent persons are analysing and seeking the meaning of emptiness. Based on that, I have commissioned the translation into English and publication of the following works:

> *The Buddhism of Tibet* and *The Key to the Middle Way*, both by myself.
> *The Precious Garland of Advice for the King*, by the protector Nāgārjuna. This good explanation is a great compendium of both the profound emptiness and the extensive deeds of compassion, illuminating as well techniques for social welfare.
> *The Song of the Four Mindfulnesses*, by Kaysang Gyatso, the Seventh Dalai Lama. This work has only a few words, but contains all the essentials of sūtra and tantra.

The present volume contains my own works, followed by the two texts by Nāgārjuna and Kaysang Gyatso.

The Buddhist monk, Tenzin Gyatso, BE 2516, AD 1972, the Tibetan Water Mouse year in the tenth month on the twelfth day.

Contents

I
The Buddhism of Tibet

TENZIN GYATSO
The Fourteenth Dalai Lama

Translated by Jeffrey Hopkins
with Anne Klein

Preface

This introduction to Tibetan Buddhism is intended for beginners. The first half is a revised version of the appendix called *An Outline of Buddhism in Tibet* in my book *My Land and My People*. The second half expounds briefly the significance of the refuge, the concordance of actions and their fruits, the three trainings and Bodhicitta.

May those who seek the path of peace and happiness find it.

The Buddhist monk Tenzin Gyatso
(The Fourteenth Dalai Lama)

The Need for Religious Practice in Our Present Lives

The reason why we should engage in religious practice is that no matter how much material progress there is, it alone cannot generate adequate and lasting pleasure. Indeed, the more we progress materially, the more we have to live in constant fear and anxiety. Through progress in new fields of knowledge we have reached the moon, which some ancient peoples regarded as a source of refuge. Although there may be instances where the resources of the moon and other planets can be utilised for the advantage of human beings, perhaps in the end such advances will make enemies outside our world. In any case, such techniques can never bring ultimate and lasting happiness to human beings. These methods induce only an external physical pleasure; therefore, even though slight mental pleasure sometimes arises due to these conditions, it cannot last. On the other hand, it is widely known that when one searches for happiness in terms only of the mind, physical hardships are easy to bear. This depends on engaging in the practice of religious methods and transforming the mind.

Furthermore, even the arising of pleasure in this life depends on religious practice. Pleasure and pain, whether great or small, do not arise from superficial external factors alone; one must have their internal causes. These are the potencies or latencies of virtuous and non-virtuous actions in the mind. These potencies are in a dormant state; they are activated when one encounters external causes, and thus feelings of pleasure or pain occur. If these potencies are absent, no matter how many external factors are present, there is no way for

15

pleasure or pain to appear or disappear. Such potencies are established by deeds done in the past.

Therefore, regardless of what form of suffering the effect takes, one initially must have done a bad deed through an undisciplined mind and thereby 'accumulated' such a deed. The deed's potency is established in the mind, and later, when one meets with certain causes, suffering is undergone. Thus, all pleasures and pains basically derive from the mind. For this reason, the mind cannot be disciplined without religious practice, and by not disciplining the mind bad actions are 'accumulated'. They in turn establish potencies in one's mental continuum, in dependence on which the fruits of suffering are produced.

The Need for Religious Practice for Our Future Lives

Although in some regions of existence beings have only minds, most sentient beings also have a physical base. Both body and mind have their direct causes, and if we illustrate this with birth from a womb, the direct cause of the body is the semen of the father and the blood of the mother. The mind likewise has a direct cause of a type similar to itself. The beginning in this life of the continuum of the mind that is of similar type to the present mind is the mind at the moment of its 'linking' to the centre of the mingled semen and blood of the parents. This mental entity must definitely have a former continuum, because external phenomena cannot become mind and mind cannot become external phenomena. If a continuum of this mental entity necessarily exists, then it definitely must be a mind before its 'linking' [to the new life]. This establishes the existence of a former life.

Because such a mind is one continuum, even nowadays there are cases of former lives being remembered by some adults and children who have all the conditions conducive to such memory. In attested biographies from the past there are also many instances of remembrance of former lives.

Although cause and effect are different, they must be related through partial similarity. For example, because a body has tangibility, shape, and colour, its direct cause must also have these qualities; and because a mind does not have shape and so forth, its direct cause cannot have these qualities either. Analogously, seeds of sweet-tasting plants create fruits that are sweet. Therefore, the parents' semen and blood, which are physical, cannot be put as the direct cause of a non-physical mind. In dependence on this and other reasons, it can definitely be concluded that former and later lives exist. Then, as former and later lives do exist, it is extremely clear that there is nothing except religious practice that is helpful for the continuum of lives. These are the reasons why religious practice is necessary.

Buddhism, One of the Many Religions of the World: Its Teacher

In this world, just as there are many medicines for a particular disease, so there are many religious systems that serve as methods for achieving happiness for all sentient beings, human and otherwise. Though each of these systems has different modes of practice and different modes of expression, I think that they are all similar in that they improve the body, speech and mind of those who practise them, and in that they all have good aims. They are all similar in teaching that bad

17

actions of speech, such as lying and divisiveness, and bad physical actions, such as stealing and killing, are improper.

It is sad that throughout history there have been instances of struggle and hatred among the followers of different religions. It would be good if these were all things in the past that would never happen again. The practitioners of religions definitely could come to agree together. At present there are, in general, the two factions of those who do and those who do not engage in religious practice; it is therefore important that practitioners be unified without bias. This is not to be done with a sense of hatred [for those who do not practise]. Not only will unity help practitioners, but also its very purpose should be to achieve temporary and lasting help and happiness for non-practitioners as well. It would serve as a method for removing their ignorance, which obscures what should be adopted and what should be discarded, and would set them on a path towards ultimate happiness. I wish to offer my hopes and prayers that all religions unite to achieve this purpose.

Books written or translated in the past have certainly done a great service to Buddhism, but some of them, other than giving only a rough treatment of the path, cannot provide the deeper significance. To remedy this situation a cultural institution called the Library of Tibetan Works and Archives has been established. Among other activities, it has undertaken the translation into English of several works from original Tibetan sources. Translation teams consisting of Tibetan and foreign scholars have been specially set up for this purpose. The present volume forms the first in the series of this project of producing translations that accord with the oral tradition and the real meaning of all the technical terms. For followers of religious systems to come together, they must be able to know and understand each other's systems, and to this end I am presenting a brief introduction to the Buddhism of Tibet.

Our teacher, Śākyamuni Buddha, is one among the thousand

Buddhas of this aeon. These Buddhas were not Buddhas from the beginning, but were once sentient beings like ourselves. How they came to be Buddhas is this. Of body and mind, mind is predominant, for body and speech are under the influence of the mind. Afflictions such as desire do not contaminate the nature of the mind, for the nature of the mind is pure, uncontaminated by any taint. Afflictions are peripheral factors of a mind, and through gradually transforming all types of defects, such as these afflictions, the adventitious taints can be completely removed. This state of complete purification is Buddhahood; therefore, Buddhists do not assert that there is any Buddha who has been enlightened from the beginning.

Buddhas are always striving for the welfare of beings migrating in cyclic existence. In every hour and minute they create limitless forms of welfare for beings through billions of emanations of their body, speech and mind. For instance, in this aeon—an aeon being a period of an extremely great number of years—they will appear in the aspect of one thousand supreme Emanation Bodies (Nirmāṇakāya) as Buddhas, and each will have his own new teaching.

The teaching of Śākyamuni Buddha is different from the teachings of the other Buddhas in that his has a union of sūtra and tantra, whereas most of the others do not have any tantra. [Śākyamuni Buddha was actually enlightened many aeons ago, but] from the point of view of common appearances his life was a display of twelve main events: his descent from the Joyous Pure Land (Tuṣita), his conception, birth, schooling, mastery in the arts, sporting with his retinue of wives, renunciation, asceticism, meditation under the tree of enlightenment, conquest of the array of evil ones, becoming a Buddha, turning the wheel of doctrine, and nirvāṇa.

Buddha's coming to this world was for the sake of beings migrating in cyclic existence. Because his miraculous exhibition of speech is chief among the three types of miraculous exhibitions [body, speech and mind], his coming was for the sake of turning the wheel of doctrine.

The teacher Śākyamuni was born in a royal family, and in the early part of his life he performed his princely duties. When he saw that all the marvels of cyclic existence are of the nature of suffering, he renounced his kingdom and began to practise asceticism. Finally, at Bodh Gayā, he displayed the ways of becoming fully enlightened. Then in stages he turned the three renowned wheels of doctrine.

In the first period, at Varaṇāsī, Buddha turned the wheel of doctrine that is based on the four noble truths; he did this mainly in consideration of those having the lineage of Hearers (Śrāvaka). In the middle period, at Gṛdhrakūṭa, he set forth the middle wheel of doctrine, which is based on the mode of non-inherent existence of all phenomena; he did this mainly in consideration of trainees of sharp faculties who bear the Mahāyāna lineage. In the final period, at Vaiśālī, he set forth the final wheel [which is based on discriminating between those phenomena that do and those that do not truly exist]; he did this mainly in consideration of trainees of middling and lower faculties who bear the Mahāyāna lineage. The teacher Buddha also appeared in the body of Vajradhara and set forth tantric doctrines.

The volumes of translations into Tibetan that are widely known nowadays as the Kangyur are solely the word of Buddha. The sūtra portion of the Blessed One's word is incorporated in the three scriptural divisions. These are arranged according to their subject matter: the discipline (vinaya) is concerned with ethics (śīla); the class of scripture (sūtrānta) with meditative stabilisation (samādhi); and knowledge (abhidharma) with wisdom (prajñā). The tantric doctrines are incorporated in the four sets of tantra. Or, in another way, the four sets of tantra can be included in the scriptural division called 'class of scripture'.

The Spread of Buddhism to Tibet

Long before Buddhism spread to Tibet the Bon religion, which came from the country of Shang-Shung, was prevalent in Tibet, and even nowadays there are lecturers and practitioners of the Bon system. Originally, it seems not to have been very extensive in scope. However, when later the Buddhist teaching spread from India and was widely disseminated in Tibet, it appears that the Bon system of assertion on view, meditation and behaviour became more vast and profound.

The Buddhist teaching first spread to Tibet during the reign of the Tibetan King Hla-to-to-ri-nyen-tsen (Lha-tho-tho-ri-gnyan-bstan). Then it gradually increased, and many famous Indian scholars, such as Śāntarakṣita and Kamalaśīla, as well as many adepts, such as Padmasaṃbhava, translated and disseminated many sūtras, tantras and commentaries. During the reign of Lang-dar-ma (gLang-dar-ma), the teaching suffered a setback for almost a decade, but revived again, starting from the eastern and western parts of Tibet. This marked the beginning of the later dissemination of Buddhism in Tibet. Many scholars, such as Rin-chen-sang-po (Rin-chen-bzang-po), met with famous Indian scholars and adepts and through hearing, thinking and meditating maintained and furthered the Conqueror's teaching. Also, many Indian scholars, such as Atīśa, came to Tibet and translated and disseminated many sūtras, tantras and commentaries. At this point, many of Tibet's own people became skilled in the doctrine and began writing the many Tibetan commentaries, and after a time not many famous Indian or Nepalese scholars came to Tibet.

Thus, the Buddhist teaching that spread to Tibet is just the stainless teaching of India and nothing else. The Tibetan lamas neither altered it nor mixed it with another religion. For example, in Tibetan commentaries, even after a brief exegesis of doctrine, a source is cited, be it the speech of Buddha himself or of another Indian scholar, and the point is settled only on this basis. As an extremely clear proof, during detailed discussions I have had with modern Indian scholars of both Buddhist and non-Buddhist philosophies they have said that even in instances where it is difficult to understand the meaning of doctrinal passages, the entire meaning is given in the Tibetan translations done many centuries ago. Not only that, but also some Indians scholars say that some passages which are difficult to understand in Sanskrit are understood more easily through looking at the Tibetan translations. On the basis of this information I think that those who, noticing the slight differences with Indian Buddhism due to locality, time, or external conditions, identify Tibetan Buddhism as 'Lamaism' specifically in the sense of its being a transformation of Buddhism are completely wrong. Also, at the present time, if one wants to know thoroughly all the views, meditations and practices of Hīnayāna and Mahāyāna, I think that one should read the Tibetan treatises with fine analysis over a long period of time. I may be wrong, so I hope that no one will take offence.

In India formerly, even though the systems of explanation of the scholars at Nālanda and those at Vikramaśīla were essentially the same, there were slight differences in their names and modes of instruction. In the same way, different names arose in Tibet due to the names of the lineages of Indian scholars and their students, localities, times and so forth; the more famous of these schools are the Nying-ma (rNying-ma), Ka-gyü (bKa'-rgyud), Sa-kya (Sa-skya) and Ge-luk (dGe-lugs). Though they are fundamentally the same, they have several differences in mode of instruction. Still, all of them are only the Conqueror's teaching of a union of sūtra and tantra.

The Meaning of *Dharma*

The word *dharma* in Sanskrit means 'that which holds'. All existents are *dharmas*, phenomena, in the sense that they hold or bear their own entity or character. Also, a religion is a *dharma* in the sense that it holds persons back or protects them from disasters. Here the term *dharma* refers to the latter definition. In rough terms, any elevated action of body, speech or mind is regarded as a *dharma* because through doing such an action one is protected or held back from all sorts of disasters. Practice of such actions is practice of *dharma*. Since this is not the time to deal at length with the topic of *dharma*, only the Buddhist *dharma* will be explained briefly here in comprehensible terms.

The Four Noble Truths

The Blessed One said, 'These are true sufferings, these are true sources, these are true cessations, these are true paths. Sufferings are to be known, their sources are to be abandoned, their cessations are to be actualised, the paths are to be cultivated. Sufferings are to be known; then, there will be no more suffering to be known. The sources of sufferings are to be abandoned; then, there will be no more sources to be abandoned. The cessations of suffering are to be actualised; then, there will be no more cessations to be actualised. The paths are to be cultivated; then, there will be no more paths to be cultivated.' These are the four noble truths in terms of their entities, requisite actions, and actions together with their effects. In explaining them, the interpretation of the Prāsaṅgika-Mādhyamika system, the highest among all Buddhist schools, will mainly be followed.

23

True sufferings are phenomena that arise from contaminated actions and afflictions and that are included within the term 'cyclic existence'. True sources are the causes producing true sufferings. True cessations are the states of extinguishment and disappearance of true sufferings and true sources. True paths are special methods for attaining true cessations.

Because true sufferings arise from true sources, true sources actually precede true sufferings. Also, through cultivating true paths, true cessations are actualised; true paths therefore, actually precede true cessations. However, the Blessed One reversed this order when he taught the four noble truths, and this is extremely important. For, if initially one recognises the sufferings, then one investigates their causes; therefore, Buddha set forth the sources of suffering after identifying the sufferings themselves. When one generates confidence in the ability to eliminate these sources, then a wish to actualise their cessation arises. Then for the sake of doing this, a wish to cultivate the paths arises; therefore, Buddha set forth the true paths after identifying true cessations.

Cyclic Existence and Sentient Beings

One might wonder, 'Since cyclic existence together with its miseries are true sufferings, what is cyclic existence?'

Cyclic existence is divided into three types by way of different types of abodes; these are a desire realm, a form realm and a formless realm. In the desire realm, beings partake of the pleasures of the 'five desirous attributes': forms, sounds, odours, tastes and tangible objects. The form realm has two parts: in the lower, beings are not attracted to external pleasures but partake of the pleasures of internal contemplation. In the higher part, beings have turned away from pleasurable feelings altogether and partake of neutral feelings. In the formless realm all forms, sounds, odours, tastes and tangible objects and the five senses for enjoying them are absent; there is only mind, and beings abide only in neutral feeling, one-pointedly and without distraction.

There are six different types of sentient beings who migrate in cyclic existence: gods, demigods, humans, hungry ghosts, animals and denizens of hells. Gods include beings in the form and formless realms as well as the six types of gods in the desire realm. Demigods are similar to gods but are mischievous and rough. Humans are those of the four 'continents' and so forth. Hungry ghosts are many types of beings who are severely deprived of food and drink. Animals are those in the ocean and those scattered about the surface of the earth. Denizens of hells are persons born in various colours and shapes through the force of and in accordance with their own previous actions.

The essential meaning of 'cyclic existence' is a process outside of one's control, that proceeds in accordance with contaminated actions and afflictions. Its essential nature is misery; its function is to provide a basis for suffering and to induce suffering in the future. Technically, cyclic existence is the contaminated mental and physical aggregates appropriated through contaminated actions and afflictions. Because there is nothing in all three realms to which cyclic existence does not apply, the mental and physical aggregates of all these beings are cyclic existences.

Causes of Cyclic Existence

What are the roots of cyclic existence? The sources of suffering are two: contaminated actions and afflictions.

Afflictions are classed as peripheral mental factors and are not themselves any of the six main minds [eye, ear, nose, tongue, body and mental consciousnesses]. However, when any of the afflicting mental factors becomes manifest, a main mind [a mental consciousness] comes under its influence, goes wherever the affliction leads it, and 'accumulates' a bad action.

There are a great many different kinds of afflictions, but the chief of them are desire, hatred, pride, wrong view and so forth. Of these, desire and hatred are chief. Because of an initial attachment to oneself, hatred arises when something undesirable occurs. Further, through being attached to oneself the pride that holds one to be superior arises, and similarly when one has no knowledge of something, a wrong view that holds the object of this knowledge to be non-existent arises.

How do self-attachment and so forth arise in such great force? Because of beginningless conditioning, the mind tightly holds to 'I, I' even in dreams, and through the power of this conception, self-attachment and so forth occur. This false conception of 'I' arises because of one's lack of knowledge concerning the mode of existence of things. The fact that all objects are empty of inherent existence is obscured and one conceives things to exist inherently; the strong conception of 'I' derives from this. Therefore, the conception that phenomena inherently exist is the afflicting ignorance that is the ultimate root of all afflictions.

Actions

From the point of view of their nature, actions are of two types: intentional and operational. An intentional action occurs prior to physical or verbal deeds and is a mental factor that provides the impulse to act. An operational action is a physical or verbal action that occurs at the time of engaging in activity.

From the point of view of the effects they impel, actions are of three types: meritorious, non-meritorious and invariable. Meritorious actions impel one to happy migrations, which are the lives of humans, demigods and gods. Non-meritorious actions impel one to bad migrations, which are the lives of animals, hungry ghosts and denizens of hells. Invariable actions impel one to the upper realms, which are those of form and the formless.

All of these can be divided into physical, verbal and mental actions. Also, from the point of view of how the effects are experienced, actions can be divided into three types: the effects of an action 'accumulated' in this life may be experienced in this very life, in the next life, or in any life beyond the next.

Liberation

Cyclic existence means bondage, and liberation means freedom from this bondage. As was explained above, the causes of cyclic existence are contaminated actions and afflictions. If the roots of the afflictions are eliminated and if new actions are not 'accumulated', since there are no afflictions to activate the predispositions of contaminated actions persisting from the past, the causes of cyclic existence have been eliminated. Then there is freedom from bondage. Some say that as long as one still has mental and physical aggregates wrought by former contaminated actions and afflictions one has a nirvāṇa with remainder. When these no longer remain, there is a nirvāṇa without remainder. 'Without remainder' means that there is no remainder of mental and physical aggregates wrought by contaminated actions and afflictions, but the continuum of consciousness and the continuum of uncontaminated mental and physical aggregates still exist.

Through removing the cause, the contaminated aggregates

27

cease, and through becoming free from them all, the suffering that depends on them is extinguished. Such is liberation, of which there are two types: a liberation that is a mere extinguishing of sufferings and their sources and the great, unsurpassed liberation, the rank of Buddhahood. The former is an extinguishment of all the afflicting obstructions [which prevent liberation from cyclic existence] but not of the obstructions to direct cognition of all objects of knowledge. The latter liberation is the ultimate rank, an utter extinguishing of both the afflictions and the obstructions to omniscience.

Hīnayāna

In order to attain either of these liberations, one must rely on a path. There are paths of ordinary beings and paths of Superiors. The latter are true paths. There are two types of Hīnayānists: Hearers (Śrāvaka) and Solitary Realisers (Pratyekabuddha). Each of them has five paths, and thus there are ten Hīnayāna paths.

Although Hearers are lower and Solitary Realisers are higher, their basis is the same. They both practise the Hīnayāna doctrine of a path that serves as a method for achieving a mere liberation from cyclic existence for their own sakes. In brief, they take as their basis a set of ethics in conjunction with a thought definitely to get out of cyclic existence. On the basis of this, they cultivate a union of calm abiding (śamatha) and special insight (vipaśyanā), which is directed toward emptiness, and thereby extricate the afflictions together with their seeds so that it is impossible for them ever to grow again. Doing this, they attain liberation.

Both Hearers and Solitary Realisers have a series of five paths: the paths of accumulation, preparation, seeing, meditation and no more learning. One who trains in such paths is called a Hīnayānist.

Mahāyāna

Mahāyānists primarily seek the rank of Buddhahood, the non-abiding nirvāṇa, the supreme liberation, for the sake of others. In conjunction with this aspiration to highest enlightenment for the sake of all sentient beings, they practise the paths that were explained above for the Hīnayāna. However, these paths are higher and more powerful because of the difference in motivation. The paths are also augmented with special methods, the main of which are the six perfections and the four means of gathering students. Based on these, Mahāyānists overcome totally and forever not only the afflicting obstructions but also the obstructions to omniscience. When the two obstructions are overcome, they attain the rank of Buddhahood.

In the Mahāyāna there are also five paths: the Mahāyāna paths of accumulation, preparation, seeing, meditation and no more learning. Though these are similar in name to the Hīnayāna paths, they in fact have a great difference. In brief, the difference between the two vehicles of Hīnayāna and Mahāyāna lies in their initial motivation, and because of this the general body of their paths, and especially their methods or deeds, come to be different. Through this, in turn, their effects also have a great difference of inferiority and superiority.

Once Hīnayānists have attained their fruit, do they remain there? Or do they enter the Mahāyāna?

They definitely do finally enter the Mahāyāna. Because their type of liberation is not the ultimate attainment, they are not satisfied with it, but gradually seek the ultimate attainment, train in its paths and become Buddhas.

Tantrayāna

The Mantra Vehicle has four sets of tantras: Action (Kriyā),

Performance (Caryā), Yoga, and Highest Yoga (Anuttara-yoga). The Highest Yoga set of tantras is superior to the lower ones. Many tens of millions of Highest Yoga tantras were set forth, but this procedure will be dealt with only briefly.

It was explained above that the various sufferings which we experience are due to the power of contaminated actions and afflictions; essentially, sufferings arise because one has been unable to tame the mind. In Highest Yoga, the methods for taming the mind are to meditate on a salutary object within the context of not allowing bad thoughts to be generated, and along with this to concentrate on important places in the body. Through these methods the Highest Yoga path is faster than the others, and this is due to the fact that the mind depends on the body. One concentrates on the various channels in which mainly blood, mainly semen, or only currents of energy [winds] flow. Then, since currents of energy cause the mind to move to objects, a yogī reverses these currents, and thus there is nothing to stir the mind; the mind does not stir or move to other objects. These are the methods that are employed in Highest Yoga.

Since such skill comes only through internal practice involving the channels and the currents of energy and not through external factors, the mind must have a strong ability to keep on its object. For the sake of acquiring this ability as well as for other reasons, the texts teach meditation on the body of a deity and so forth. The many images of deities in tantra are not arbitrary creations; they are means of purifying the impure mental and physical aggregates (skandha), the types (dhātu) and the sources (āyatana). Also the peaceful and wrathful aspects, the numbers of faces and hands, the number of principal and surrounding figures and so forth are due to differences in the trainees' dispositions, thoughts and faculties.

In brief, although there are definitely instances of achievements among these paths through the power of belief, these paths are mostly achieved through the power of reasoning. If one trains in the paths correctly and gradually, there are many reasons one can find to facilitate the attainment of conviction and a well-founded belief.

The Two Truths

Among the paths mentioned above, the paths of Superiors are true paths; the others are as if precursors to these. All the paths are included within method and wisdom. Method and wisdom, in turn, depend on the two truths. Nāgārjuna's *Fundamental Text Called 'Wisdom' (Prajñā-nāma-mūla-madhyamakakārikā,* XXIV. 8) says:

> Doctrines taught by the Buddhas
> Rely wholly on the two truths,
> Conventional worldly truths
> And truths that are ultimate.

Also, the attainment of a Truth Body (Dharmakāya) and a Form Body (Rūpakāya) on the effect stage, which is Buddhahood, depends on the practice of method and wisdom while on the path. Method and wisdom, in turn, depend on the two truths which represent the mode of being of the ground or basis [of practice]. Thus, understanding the two truths is very important, and it is a very difficult topic. The many differences in the Buddhist schools of tenets are due to their different presentations of the two truths.

Let us speak here a little about the two truths in accordance with the Prāsaṅgika-Mādhyamika system. All phenomena that we manifestly perceive have two modes of being. One is the nominal or conventional entity of the phenomenon, and the other is its final mode of being, its emptiness of inherent existence. Let us give an example from another sphere; a pen, for instance, has a gross mode of being which can be seen by the ordinary eye and also has a mode of being which cannot be seen by the ordinary eye and which is the fact of its being a mass of atoms.

What are the individual meanings of 'ultimate truth' and 'conventional truth?'

In rough and brief terms, an object found by a valid cogniser distinguishing a final nature is an ultimate truth and an object found by a valid cogniser distinguishing a conventionality is a conventional truth. Therefore, emptinesses and true cessations are ultimate truths, and everything else are conventional truths.

All of these phenomena have some mode of dependence; either they arise, change and cease in dependence on causes, or they are posited in dependence on a continuum, or in dependence on their parts and so forth. No matter what type of dependent phenomena they are, they exist only in dependence on another. Not even one among them is able to stand by itself. Therefore all of them are empty of their own inherent existence. Nevertheless, all agents, actions and objects are conventionally valid. In brief, because phenomena are empty of inherent existence, they change from one thing into another, and because phenomena exist conventionally, there is good and bad, and help and harm.

A General Outline of the Practice of Buddhism

The designation 'practising a religious system' is not given to mere physical change, living in a monstery, or recitation, but it still is not definite that these could not become religious practice. In any case, religious practice must be carried out in terms of one's own thought. If one knows how to bring the teachings into one's own thought, all physical and verbal deeds can be made to accord with practice. If one does not know how to bring them into one's own thought, even though one might meditate, recite scriptures, or spend one's life in a temple, it will not help; thought is therefore important for practice. Thus, taking refuge in the Three Jewels (Buddha, his Doctrine and the Spiritual Community), taking into account the relationship between actions and their effects, and generating an attitude of helping others, are most important.

Formerly in Tibet there was a famous lama called Drom. One day Drom saw a man walking around a reliquary. 'Walking around a reliquary is good,' he said. 'Practice is even better.'

The man thought, 'Then, reading a holy book would be good.' He did so, and one day while he was reading, Drom saw him and said, 'Reading a holy book is good; practice is even better.'

The man thought, 'This also does not seem to be sufficient. Now if I do some meditation, that will certainly be practice.'

Drom saw him in meditation and said, 'Meditation is good; practice is even better.' The man was amazed and asked, 'How does one practise?' Drom answered, 'Do not be attached to this life; cause your mind to become the practices.' Drom said this because practice depends on thought.

A Specific Outline of the Practice of Buddhism

There are great advantages if one renounces this life and performs the practices. In Tibet there are many people who have renounced the world and have attained an indescribable mental and physical happiness. All the pleasures that are achieved through cherishing this life and which require many types of continuous effort do not equal even a fraction of this happiness. Nevertheless, this practice is difficult for most people to undertake.

What is the mode of practice for the majority of people? In general, immoral livelihood requiring deceit, lying and so forth is the opposite of religious practice and thus is not compatible with it. However, in harmony with religious practice, one can engage in a livelihood that accords with the respectable ways of the world, such as administering a government, promoting economic measures, or taking any steps towards securing the welfare and enjoyment of others. These should be done within the context of always retaining thoughts of religious practice. It is said:

> If one practises, liberation is present even while living in a
>   household
> As in the case of the kings and ministers of India and Tibet
>   and others such as Marpa.
> If one does not practise, the causes of a bad migration are
>   present even while living in a mountain retreat
> Like a woodchuck hibernating in a hole in the ground.

The Three Refuges

What are the methods for causing one's own mind to become the practices?

Initially, one should take refuge and think about actions and their effects. The refuge is the Three Jewels: Buddha, his Doctrine and the Spiritual Community.

When a sentient being purifies the taints of his own mind as well as their latent predispositions, he is free of all defects that act as obstructions. Thus, he simultaneously and directly knows all phenomena. Such a being is called a Buddha, and he is a teacher of refuge, like a physician.

The Doctrine jewel is the superior (ārya) paths—the chief right paths which remove the taints as well as their latent predispositions—and the absences which are states of having removed what is to be removed. The Doctrine is the actual refuge, like medicine.

The Community jewel is all persons, whether lay or ordained, who have generated a superior path in their continuum. They are friends helping one to achieve refuge, like nurses.

The three refuges that have been achieved and presently exist in other beings' continuums are one's own causal refuge; one relies on a protector just as a weak person takes refuge in a stronger person. The three refuges that one will attain in the future are one's own effect refuge. One who relies on the Three Jewels from the point of view of knowing that he is to attain them, must cause them to be generated in his own continuum.

Any effect, whether good or bad, must arise in dependence on causes and conditions. Thus, at present one must actually achieve in one's own continuum the causes that are similar in type to a Doctrine jewel, the actual refuge. Therefore, one must practise the paths that are included in the three trainings (triśikṣā) in higher ethics (adhiśīla), in higher meditative stabilisation (adhisamādhi), and in higher wisdom (adhiprajñā).

Training in Higher Ethics

Even though the training in ethics takes many forms, the ethics of abandoning the ten non-virtues is their basis. Of the ten non-virtues, three pertain to bodily actions, four to verbal actions and three to mental actions. The three physical non-virtues are:

1 Taking the life of a living being: ranging from killing an insect to killing a human.

2 Stealing: taking away another's property without his consent, regardless of its value, whether the deed is done by oneself or through another.

3 Sexual misconduct: committing adultery.

The four verbal non-virtues are:

4 Lying: deceiving others through spoken words or physical gestures.

5 Divisiveness: creating dissension by causing those in agreement to disagree or by causing those in disagreement to disagree even further.

6 Harshness: abusing others.

7 Senselessness: talking about foolish things motivated by desire and so forth.

The three mental non-virtues are:

8 Covetousness: thinking, 'May this become mine', desiring something that belongs to another.

9 Harmful intent: wishing to injure others, be it great or small injury.

10 Wrong view: viewing some existent thing, such as rebirth, cause and effect, or the Three Jewels, as non-existent.

The opposites of these ten non-virtues are the ten virtues, and engaging in them is called the practice of ethics.

Training in Higher Meditative Stabilisation

Then, how does one progress in the training of meditative stabilisation, which is the mind's abiding one-pointedly on its object?

There are many types of meditative stabilisation, but let us explain calm abiding (śamatha) here. The nature of calm abiding is the one-pointed abiding on any object without distraction of a mind conjoined with a bliss of physical and mental pliancy. If it is supplemented with taking refuge, it is a Buddhist practice, and if it is supplemented with an aspiration to highest enlightenment for the sake of all sentient beings, it is a Mahāyāna practice. Its merits are that, if one has achieved calm abiding, one's mind and body are pervaded by joy and bliss; one can—through the power of its mental and physical pliancy—set the mind on any virtuous object one chooses; and many special qualities such as clairvoyance and emanations are attained.

The main purpose and advantage of calm abiding are that through it one can achieve special insight (vipaśyanā), which realises emptiness, and can thereby be liberated from cyclic existence. Also, most of the secondary beneficial attributes of the three vehicles (Hīnayāna, Mahāyāna and Tantrayāna) arise in dependence on calm abiding. The benefits are many.

One should have all the following causal collections for the achievement of calm abiding. The place where one practices should be free of noise, since noise is a thorn to concentration; the area and water should be congenial. The meditator himself should have few wants, know satisfaction, be free from the din and bustle of the world, and should avoid non-virtuous physical and verbal deeds. Through hearing and thinking he should have eliminated misconceptions about the subjects of meditation, he should know how to reflect on the faults of desire, on the meaning of impermanence and so on.

With regard to the actual practice of calm abiding, Maitreya says in his *Discrimination of the Middle Way and the Extremes* (*Madhyāntavibhaṅga*):

> The cause of its arising is to observe the relinquishing
> Of the five faults and the application of the eight antidotes.

The five faults to be relinquished are:

1 Laziness: not wishing to cultivate meditative stabilisation.
2 Forgetfulness: not remembering the object of meditation.
3 Lethargy and excitement: interruptions of meditative stabilisation.
4 Non-application of the antidotes: occurring when lethargy and excitement arise.
5 Over-application: continuing to apply the antidotes even though lethargy and excitement have been extinguished.

The eight antidotes are the means for relinquishing these faults. The antidotes to laziness are:

1 Faith: seeing the good qualities of meditative stabilisation.
2 Aspiration: seeking to attain those good qualities.
3 Effort: delighting in engaging in meditative stabilisation.
4 Physical and mental pliancy: an effect [of effort].

The antidote to forgetfulness is:

5 Mindfulness: maintaining concentration on an object continuously.

The antidote to lethargy and excitement is:

6 Awareness: knowing that lethargy or excitement has arisen or is arising.

The antidote to non-application is:

7 Application: engaging in the antidotes to lethargy or excitement.

The antidote to over-application is:

8 Desisting from application: relaxing one's effort.

Through applying the eight antidotes the five faults are gradually eliminated, and one passes through nine states of concentration.

1 Setting the mind: collecting the mind and aiming it at an internal object [such as the visualised form of Buddha].

2 Continually setting: prolonging concentration on the object more than in the previous state.

3 Re-setting: immediately recognising distraction and returning to the object.

4 Increased setting: collecting the mind from concentrating on the gross [aspects of the visualised object of meditation] and setting it more and more steadily on the subtle [details of the object].

5 Disciplining: knowing the good qualities of meditative stabilisation and taking joy in them.

6 Pacifying: ceasing dislike for meditative stabilisation.

7 Thorough pacifying: through effort relinquishing even subtle lethargy and excitement just after they arise.

8 Making one-pointed: generating meditative stabilisation continuously within the context of its being impossible for the non-conducive to interrupt the process.

9 Putting in equipoise: spontaneously fixing on the object of meditation without requiring the effort of relying on mindfulness and awareness.

The above nine states of concentration are accomplished by means of the six powers. The first state is accomplished through the power of hearing, the second through the power of thinking, and the third and fourth through the power of mindfulness. The fifth and sixth are accomplished through the power of awareness, the seventh and eighth through the power of effort, and the ninth through the power of familiarity.

The periods of the four mental activities [which are ways in which the mind engages its object] occur during the nine states of concentration:

1 Forcibly fixing: during the first and second states the mind is strenuously fixed on its object of concentration.

2 Interruptedly fixing: from the third to the seventh state concentration occurs intermittently.
3 Non-interruptedly fixing: during the eighth state the mind is capable of staying on its object without interruption.
4 Effortlessly fixing: during the ninth state the mind spontaneously remains on its object.

If one knows the nature, order and distinctions of the levels explained above without error and cultivates calm abiding, one can easily generate faultless meditative stabilisation in about a year.

This has been a treatment of the topic of calm abiding that applies to objects in general. In particular, if one cultivates calm abiding taking the mind itself as the object, additional advantages are found. One identifies one's own mind. The mind is as vacuous as space, not having any physical qualities such as form or shape. It is something that merely perceives whatever aspects of an object appear to it with vivid clarity. Once the mind has been identified to be like this, one then engages in the nine states, the relinquishing of the five faults, the application of the eight antidotes and so forth, as has been explained above in the discussion of objects in general. One thus cultivates calm abiding.

This has been a mere enumeration of the elements of calm abiding in the sense of my having made an extreme abbreviation of Maitreya's and Asaṅga's instructions. The measure of having achieved calm abiding is that once physical and then mental pliancy have been achieved, one attains a pliancy of immovability, which is the mind's abiding one-pointedly on its object. At that time one achieves an actual calm abiding which is included in the preparation stage for the first concentration. Of the three realms, this concentration belongs to the form realm. Having attained calm abiding, the mind is serviceable, and no matter on what type of virtuous object or meaning it is set, the mind remains there one-pointedly.

Through the force of this, the ability of the mind to comprehend a meaning is very great.

Training in Higher Wisdom

How then does one progress in the training of wisdom?

In general, there are five types of wisdom, but the chief are the wisdom that cognises conventionalities, or the knowledge of nominalities, and the wisdom that cognises the ultimate, or the knowledge of the mode of being. Each of these has numerous aspects, but the wisdom to be discussed here is the one that, when generated in one's mental continuum, can completely overcome the afflicting obstructions and the obstructions to omniscience.

What is emptiness, the object of this wisdom?

Emptiness is the final mode of being of all phenomena. It does not, for instance, arise through the compassionate activities of Buddhas or through the actions of sentient beings. Each and every phenomenon, from the very fact of its coming into existence, is established as having the nature of emptiness. In a sūtra it says, 'Whether the Tathāgatas appear or not, the nature and reality of phenomena just abides.'

What is the mode of being of phenomena?

Candrakīrti's commentary on Āryadeva's *Four Hundred* says, 'Here, "self" is an inherent existence (svabhāva) of phenomena, that is, a non-dependence on another. The non-existence of this [type of self] is selflessness.' Thus, inherent existence is the object of negation, and a mere negative of inherent existence is called an emptiness.

How does one ascertain such an emptiness?

Although all phenomena have always had a nature of emptiness, we have been unable to cognise them as such. The method for cognising the meaning of emptiness is to ascertain an emptiness through relying on the Mādhyamika style of reasoning. In general, the nature or mode of being of phenomena and the way that they appear to our mind are opposite and contradictory. Though the mode of being of phenomena is that they do not inherently exist, because of beginningless conditioning to the conception of inherent existence, whatever phenomena appear to our minds appear to exist inherently, and we conceive them as existing inherently. Because, on the basis of this, the way that phenomena appear to our minds and their actual mode of being are opposite, their mode of appearance to our minds and our mode of adhering are totally fallacious. In particular, a consciousness conceiving inherent existence is a wrong consciousness that is mistaken with respect to its referent object. Therefore, one should gain conviction that the referent object of the mind—a mind that, until now, very forcefully assented to this false appearance of inherent existence, thinking, 'This truly exists'—is nonexistent. Once the referent object of the conception of inherent existence is known to be non-existent, one can easily ascertain emptiness, the mode of being of all phenomena, that is, their non-inherent existence.

With respect to this, it is initially important to ascertain how our mind misconceives [the nature of things]. To us beginners, each and every phenomenon appears to exist inherently. For instance, when one thinks to oneself, 'I, I', a self-sufficient 'I' appears, as if it were totally unrelated, different from, or independent of one's own body, mind, collection of mental and physical aggregates and continuum. If one clearly ascertains this mode of appearance and mode of adherence to the appearance, then one should analyse as follows. If this 'I' existed the way it appears, as if it were completely independent of one's own mental and physical aggregates, types, and sources, would it be one with the aggregates or different from them?

If the 'I' and the mental and physical aggregates were the

same, there would be no way to make the many divisions of
the aggregates, types, sources and so forth; the aggregates
would have to be one [like the 'I']. Or, just as there are
aggregates, types and sources, so there would have to be many
'I's'. Furthermore, when the form aggregates of this life, for
instance, are destroyed, the 'I' would also have to be destroyed.
Thus, there is no way that the 'I' and the aggregates can be
one.

Also, if the 'I' and aggregates were self-sufficiently different,
they would be different in the sense that the one would not
depend on the other. Then, when my body is sick, it would
not mean that 'I' am sick, and when my stomach is full, it
would not mean that 'I' am full. However, this is not the case.
My body's being sick means that 'I' am sick and that suffering
arises in the mind. Thus, there is no way that the 'I' and the
mental and physical aggregates could be unrelatedly different.

Further, apart from sameness or difference, there is no
other mode of subsistence of the 'I' and the aggregates. For,
once there is an 'I' which, in accordance with its appearance,
exists as if it were inherently existent, it must be either one
with the aggregates or different from the aggregates. There is
not at all any way of subsistence other than as one of these two.

Based on this, because the 'I' that so agreeably appears to
our minds to be inherently existent is not the same as one's
own aggregates and is not different from them, such an 'I'
does not exist at all. Through ascertaining its non-existence
thus, it is understood that on the one hand such an 'I' as
presently appears to our minds does not exist, but on the other
hand the 'I' is not totally non-existent. Conventionally, a
merely imputedly existent 'I', a nominality, remains. This
imputedly existent 'I' which is a mere nominality, can achieve
resources, such as food and drink, and can own and use things,
such as clothing. This 'I', which is the wanderer in cyclic
existence, the practitioner of religion and the attainer of
liberation, can be presented easily, without the least difficulty.

It is, therefore, free of the four extremes, which are: inherent existence, total non-existence, both of these, and neither of them. Nāgārjuna says in his *Fundamental Text Called 'Wisdom'* (XV. 10):

'Existence' is a holding to permanence,
'Non-existence' is a view of nihilism.

And:

Not existent, not non-existent, not both
And not something that is not both.

When the 'I' is ascertained as being free of the four extremes and as only imputedly existent, that is, a mere nominality, then one has ascertained a subtle selflessness relative to the 'I' as a base of selflessness. One should then switch the reasoning to other things and apply it to one's eyes and so forth, to external phenomena such as forms, sounds, tastes and odours, and even to emptiness itself. Through reasoning, it can be proved that all phenomena do not exist independently.

With respect to the meaning of all phenomena not being inherently existent, one should first hear about emptiness from reading the great books in depth; and then, in dependence on hearing about it from others, one generates the wisdom that arises from hearing. Then, in dependence on thinking again and again about its meaning, one generates the wisdom that arises from thinking. When one has gained lengthy familiarity with one-pointed meditation on the meaning that has been deeply ascertained, the wisdom that arises from meditation is attained. This occurs when the capacity of one's mind is extremely powerful through having formerly achieved calm abiding and one abides one-pointedly on the meaning of emptiness. A bliss of physical and mental pliancy is generated at this time, just as it was on the occasion of calm abiding. The difference is that the bliss of mental and physical pliancy on the occasion of calm abiding is induced by the force of stabilising meditation, but now a bliss of mental and physical pliancy that is induced by the power of analysis is generated. When this special meditative stabilisation, conjoined with such bliss, is achieved, one attains special insight. Since this special insight arises within the context of emptiness being the object, it is a meditative stabilisation that is a union of calm abiding and special insight apprehending emptiness.

At that point one has generated the sign of the path of preparation which was explained above. Further, when one cognises emptiness directly for the first time, the path of seeing is attained, and step by step the intellectually acquired and innate obstructions are removed. Finally, one is able to overcome completely and forever the afflicting obstructions and the obstructions to omniscience as well as their latent predispositions.

This has been an extremely brief account of how to practise the training of wisdom. In terms of superiority and inferiority, the succeeding trainings are superior to those that precede them. However, in terms of the order of their generation in one's continuum, the former trainings are like a basis or support for generating the latter, and therefore the training in ethics is most important in the beginning.

If one proceeds in the paths of the three trainings, taking as a basis the proper practice of refuge as well as understanding actions and their effects, the rank of liberation can be obtained. If, in addition to these, the precious mind of enlightenment (bodhicitta), which is induced by love and mercy, is cultivated and if one then practises the three trainings in conjunction with an aspiration for highest enlightenment for the sake of all sentient beings, the rank of omniscience, the superior liberation, can be obtained.

The Mind of Enlightenment

How is the mind of enlightenment cultivated?

One must consider not one's own welfare alone but the welfare of all sentient beings. Like oneself, all sentient beings are afflicted by suffering; thus, even the smallest insect is similar to oneself in not wanting suffering and wanting happiness. Although sentient beings do not want suffering, they do not know how to forsake it, and although they want happiness, they do not know how to achieve it. Since they are unable to do this by themselves, one must become able oneself to free sentient beings from suffering as well as from its causes and establish them in a state of happiness.

There is no way to forsake suffering and achieve happiness other than for the causes, which exist in the continuums of sentient beings and which give rise to suffering, to be removed and for the causes of happiness to be achieved in their own continuums. The Blessed One said:

> Buddhas neither wash sins away with water,
> Nor remove beings' sufferings with their hands,
> Nor transfer their realisations to others; beings
> Are freed through the teachings of the truth, the nature of
> things.

There is no way to remove sins in the way that grime is washed away with water or to remove suffering like picking out a thorn. There is no way for a Buddha to transfer the realisations in his own continuum and give them to others. Then, how is suffering removed? Sentient beings are liberated from all suffering in dependence on the teachings of reality, the mode of being of phenomena.

Thus, sentient beings are freed through teaching them what is to be adopted and what is to be discarded. In order to teach sentient beings what is to be adopted and what is to be discarded, one must first know and understand these oneself. Also, there is no one other than a Buddha who is able to teach paths without error in accordance with the various dispositions, thoughts and interests, not just of a few sentient beings but of all. Since this is so, one is certain to attain the rank of Buddhahood as a conducive circumstance for achieving one's aim, the welfare of sentient beings. For example, if a man is stricken with thirst, his thirst is mainly removed by drinking water and so forth. Yet, he must first seek a vessel in which to drink the water. Similarly, here also, although one's main purpose is to liberate sentient beings from suffering as well as its causes, in order to do this one must first develop an aspiration to achieve the rank of highest enlightenment from seeing the necessity for doing so.

If such an attitude is generated, it is called a mind of enlightenment, an aspiration to highest enlightenment for the sake of all sentient beings. If in conjunction with such an attitude one engages in virtues, great or small, such as meditating on emptiness, cultivating calm abiding, taking refuge, forsaking killing, these virtuous deeds—when they are conjoined with this altruistic attitude—naturally become causes of omniscience.

II
The Key to
the Middle Way

A Treatise on the Realisation
of Emptiness

TENZIN GYATSO
The Fourteenth Dalai Lama

Translated by Jeffrey Hopkins and
Lati Rimpoche
with Alexander Berzin, Jonathan Landaw
and Anne Klein

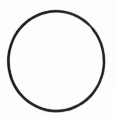

Translators' Note

The text was translated by Jeffrey Hopkins, who orally re-translated the English into Tibetan for verification and correction by Lati Rimpoche and then worked with Alexander Berzin, Jonathan Landaw, and Anne Klein to improve the presentation in English.

The Key to the Middle Way

Homage to the perfection of wisdom.

> I respectfully bow down to the Conqueror,
> Protector of all beings through boundless compassion,
> With dominion over glorious wisdom and deeds, but who
> Like an illusion is only designated by words and thoughts.

> I will explain here in brief terms the essence
> Of the ambrosia of his good speech,
> The mode of the union of emptiness and dependent-arising,
> To increase the insight of those with burgeoning intellect.

We all want happiness and do not want suffering. Moreover, achieving happiness and eliminating suffering depend upon the deeds of body, speech and mind. As the deeds of body and speech depend upon the mind, we must therefore constructively transform the mind. The ways of constructively transforming the mind are to cause mistaken states of consciousness not to be generated and good states of consciousness to be both generated and increased.

What are the determinants, in this context, of a bad state of consciousness? A state of consciousness, once produced, may initially cause ourselves to become unhappy and our previously calm mind suddenly to become excited or tense. This may then act as the cause of hard breathing, nervous sweating, illness, and so forth. From these, in turn, bad deeds of body and speech may arise, which directly or indirectly may also cause hardship for others. All states of consciousness that give rise to such a causal sequence are assigned as bad. The determinants of good states of consciousness, on the other hand, are just the opposite. All states of consciousness that cause the bestowal of the fruit of happiness and peace upon ourselves or others, either superficially or in depth, are assigned as good.

As for ways of causing mistaken states of consciousness not to be generated, there are such means as undergoing brain operations, ingesting various types of drugs, making our awareness dull as if overcome with drowsiness, and making ourselves senseless as if in deep sleep. However, apart from only occasional superficial help, these mostly do more harm than good from the point of view of deep solutions.

Therefore, the way of beneficially transforming the mind is as follows. First we must think about the disadvantages of bad states of consciousness, identifying them from our own personal experience. Then we must recognise the good states of consciousness. If familiarity with them is developed through thinking again and again about their advantages and about their supporting validators, then the various types of good states of consciousness will become stronger. This occurs through the force of familiarity and through these good states of consciousness having valid foundations and being qualities dependent on the mind [and thus capable of limitless development]. Then, it is natural that the defective states of consciousness will decrease in strength. Thereby, in time, sure signs of goodness will appear in the mind.

Many such different methods of transforming the mind have been taught by the many great teachers of this world, in accordance with individual times and places and in accordance with the minds of individual trainees. Among these, many methods of taming the mind have been taught in the books of the Buddhists. From among these, a little will be said here about the view of emptiness.

Views of selflessness are taught in both Buddhist vehicles, the Mahāyāna and the Hīnayāna, and with respect to the Mahāyāna in both sūtra and tantra divisions. When a Buddhist and a non-Buddhist are differentiated by way of behaviour, the difference is whether or not the person takes refuge in the

Three Jewels. When they are differentiated by way of view, the difference is whether or not the person asserts the views which are the four seals testifying to a doctrine's being the word of the Buddha. The four seals are:

All products are impermanent.
All contaminated things are miserable.
All phenomena are empty and selfless.
Nirvāṇa is peace.

Therefore, all Buddhists assert that all phenomena are empty and selfless.

With respect to the meaning of selflessness, there is a selflessness of persons, that is the non-existence of persons as substantial entities or self-sufficient entities. This is asserted by all four Buddhist schools of tenets: Vaibhāṣika, Sautrāntika, Cittamātra and Mādhyamika. The Cittamātrins assert, in addition, a selflessness of phenomena that is an emptiness of objects and subjects as different entities. The Mādhyamikas assert a selflessness of phenomena that is an emptiness of inherent existence.

The meaning of the views of the lower and higher schools of tenets differs greatly in coarseness and subtlety. However, if understanding is developed with respect to the lower systems, this serves as a means of deep ascertainment of the higher views; therefore, it is very helpful to do so. Here, selflessness is to be discussed in accordance with the Mādhyamika system, and within the division of the Mādhyamika into Svātantrika and Prāsaṅgika, in accordance with the Prāsaṅgika system.

Question: Did the Blessed One set forth all these different schools of tenets? If he did, on what sūtras do each rely? Also, does the difference of status and depth of the schools of tenets necessarily depend on scriptural authority?

Answer: The different views of the four schools of tenets were set forth by the Blessed One himself in accordance with the mental capacities of his trainees, whether superior, middling, or low. Some trainees were likely to fall into views of nihilism or were in danger of losing faith if taught selflessness. For them Buddha even taught the existence of a self in some sūtras. Also, some trainees were likely to go either to the extreme of eternity or to the extreme of annihilation if Buddha answered their questions in the positive or the negative. For them Buddha did not say either 'exists' or 'does not exist', but remained silent, as in the case of the fourteen inexpressible views. Also, with respect to the modes of selflessness, Buddha set forth many forms as was briefly explained above.

The sūtras on which each of the schools relies are as follows. The Vaibhāṣika and Sautrāntika schools of tenets rely mainly on the sūtras of the first wheel of doctrine, such as the *Sūtra on the Four Truths* (*Catuḥsatya*). The Cittamātra school of tenets relies mainly on the sūtras of the last wheel of doctrine, such as the *Unravelling of the Thought Sūtra* (*Saṃdhinirmocana*). The Mādhyamika school relies mainly on the sūtras of the middle wheel of doctrine, such as the *Hundred Thousand Stanza Perfection of Wisdom Sūtra* (*Śatasāhasrikāprajñāpāramitā*). There are ways of presenting the three series of wheels of doctrine from the point of view of place, time, subject and trainee [but this is not a place for such a lengthy discussion].

If it were necessary to differentiate the status and depth of the schools' different views in dependence on scriptural authority, then, since the individual sūtras each say that the system which it teaches is the superior system, we may wonder which scripture should be held as true. If one scripture were held to be true, we would then wonder how the other discordant sūtras should be considered. But, if the modes of truth of one sūtra and the non-truth of the others were necessarily provable only by scriptural authority, then the process would be endless. Therefore, the differentiation of the superiority and inferiority of views must rely only on reasoning.

Thus, the Mahāyāna sūtras say that it is necessary to

distinguish what requires interpretation and what is definitive. Thinking of this, Buddha says in a sūtra:

Monks and scholars should
Well analyse my words,
Like gold [to be tested through] melting, cutting and polishing,
And then adopt them, but not for the sake of showing me respect.

In his *Ornament of the Mahāyāna Sūtras* (*Mahāyānasūtrālaṃkāra*), Maitreya commented well on the meaning of Buddha's thought in that statement and set forth the four reliances:

1 One should not rely on the person of a teacher, but on the tenets or doctrines that he teaches.
2 One should not rely merely on the euphony and so forth of his words, but on their meaning.
3 With respect to the meaning, one should not rely on those teachings that require interpretation. Such interpretation would be necessary if there were some other non-explicit base in the teacher's thought, if there were a purpose for the teaching's being stated in interpretable form, and if the explicit words of the teaching were susceptible to refutation. One should rely, rather, on those teachings that have definitive meaning, that is, which do not require interpretation.
4 With respect to the definitive meaning, one should not rely on a dualistic consciousness, but on a non-conceptual wisdom.

With respect to a non-conceptual wisdom that apprehends a profound emptiness, one first cultivates a conceptual consciousness that apprehends an emptiness, and when a clear perception of the object of meditation arises, this becomes a non-conceptual wisdom. Moreover, the initial generation of that conceptual consciousness must depend solely on a correct reasoning. Fundamentally, therefore, this process traces back solely to a reasoning, which itself must fundamentally trace back to valid experiences common to ourselves and others. Thus, it is the thought of Dignāga and Dharmakīrti, the kings of reasoning, that fundamentally a reasoning derives from an obvious experience.

Question: For the sake of improving the mind what is the use of developing valid cognisers and states of consciousness that realise the presentations of views of emptiness? What practitioners need is a sense of practical application and goodness; it is the scholars who need to be learned.

Answer: There are many stages in the improvement of the mind. There are some in which analysis of reasons is not necessary, such as when trusting faith alone is to be cultivated single-pointedly. Not much strength, however, is achieved by just that alone. Especially for developing the mind into limitless goodness, it is not sufficient merely to familiarise the mind with its object of meditation. The object of meditation must involve reasoning. Further, it is not sufficient for the object to have reasons in general; the meditator himself must know them and have found a conviction in them. Therefore, it is impossible for the superior type of practitioner not to have intelligence.

Still, if we were forced to choose between a sense of practical application and learnedness, a sense of practical application would be more important, for one who has this will receive the full benefit of whatever he knows. The mere learnedness of one whose mind is not tamed can produce and increase bad states of consciousness, which cause unpleasantness for himself and others instead of the happiness and peace of mind that were intended. One could become jealous of those higher than oneself, competitive with equals and proud and contemptuous towards those lower and so forth. It is as if medicine had become poison. Because such danger is great, it is very important to have a composite of learnedness, a sense of practical application and goodness, without having learnedness destroy the sense of practical application or having the sense of practical application destroy learnedness.

Concerning the improvement of the mind, in order to ascertain the meaning of a selflessness or of an emptiness, it is necessary to ascertain first the meaning of just what a phenomenon is empty of when we refer to 'an emptiness'. The Bodhisattva Śāntideva says in his *Engaging in the Bodhisattva Deeds* (*Bodhicaryāvatāra*, IX.140):

> Without identifying the imputed thing
> Its non-existence cannot be apprehended.

Just so, without ascertaining that of which a phenomenon is empty, an understanding of its emptiness does not develop.

Question: Of what is it that a phenomenon is empty?

Answer: [When we Prāsaṅgikas speak of an emptiness, we are not referring to the situation in which one object is empty of some other existent entity. Thus] though we may commonly speak of an 'empty rainbow', since the rainbow is empty of anything tangible, this type of an emptiness is not what we have in mind. [This is because anything tangible can exist separate from an empty rainbow; and, moreover, there is still something positive about this rainbow empty of anything tangible, such as its having colour.] Though we may also speak of 'empty space', since space is empty of anything physical, this too is not an example of what we mean by an emptiness [although here there is nothing else positive implied about space, which is the mere absence of anything physical. This is because here too anything physical can exist separate from empty space.] Rather, when we speak of a phenomenon as being empty, we are referring to its being empty of its own inherent existence [which does not exist at all, let alone exist separate from the phenomenon. In one respect, then, there is a

57

similarity here in that just as a rainbow is naturally empty of anything tangible—it never has been tangible—so too, a phenomenon is naturally empty of its own inherent existence—it never has had inherent existence.] Further, it is not that the object of the negation [inherent existence] formerly existed and is later eliminated, like the forest which existed yesterday and which is burned by fire today, with the result that the area is now empty of the forest. Rather, this is an emptiness of an object of negation [inherent existence], which from beginning-less time has never been known validly to exist.

Also, with respect to the way in which a phenomenon is empty of the object of negation, it is not like a table top being empty of flowers. [There, the object of the negation, flowers, is an entity separate from the base of the negation, the table top. With the object of the negation being inherent existence, however, we are not negating an entity separate from the base of the negation, a phenomenon, but rather we are negating a mode of existence of the base of the negation itself. Thus] we mean that the base of the negation, a phenomenon, does not exist in the manner of the object of the negation, its own inherent existence. Therefore, without ascertaining just what the object of the negation is of which phenomena are empty, that is, without ascertaining the measure of what self is in the theory of selflessness, we cannot understand the meaning of an emptiness. A mere vacuity without any sense of 'The object of the negation is this' and 'It is not that' is utterly not the meaning of an emptiness.

Question: What is the use of going to all the trouble of first understanding what something definitely non-existent [inherent existence] would mean if it were existent; and then, after that, viewing it as definitely non-existent?

Answer: It is common worldly knowledge that by believing untrue information to be true we fall into confusion and are harmed. Similarly, by believing phenomena to be inherently existent when in fact they are not inherently existent, we are also harmed. For example, with respect to the different ways in which there can be a consciousness of 'I', there is a definite difference between the way the 'I' is apprehended when desire, hatred, pride and so forth are generated based on this 'I', and the way the 'I' is apprehended when we are relaxed without any of those attitudes being manifest. Similarly, there is the mere consciousness that apprehends an article in a store before we buy it, and there is the consciousness apprehending that article after it has been bought, when it is adhered to as 'mine' and grasped with attachment. Both these consciousnesses have the same object, and in both cases the mode of appearance of the article is the appearance of it as inherently existent. However, there is the difference of the presence or absence of our adhering to it as inherently or independently existent.

Also, when we see ten men, just from merely seeing them it appears to us that ten men exist there objectively or inherently; however, there is no certainty that we will go on to adhere at that time to this appearance of ten objectively or inherently existent men and posit truth to it. [If we were to posit truth to the appearance of these men as being inherently existent, the process of doing so would be as follows.] For either right or wrong reasons, a strong thought [based on having conceived these ten men to be inherently existent] will be generated, which incorrectly considers one from among these ten men as good or bad. At that time, our intellect will falsely superimpose on the appearance of this man a goodness or badness that exceeds what actually exists. Desire and hatred will then be generated, and consequently we will adhere at that time to this object [the appearance of an inherently existent good or bad man] tightly from the depths of our mind as true, most true.

Therefore, a consciousness conceiving inherent existence precedes any bad consciousness, leading it on by the nose, and also accompanies, or aids, many other bad consciousnesses as well. Thus, if there were no ignorance conceiving inherent existence, then there would be no chance for desire, hatred and so forth to be generated. Since that is so, it is important to identify the beginningless emptiness of the object of the negation, which is to say, it is important to identify as non-existent that non-existent entity [inherent existence] which has never validly been known to exist. Once we have made this identification, it is necessary to generate conviction in it as well. The purpose of this process is to cease the arising of incorrect thoughts, inexhaustible like ripples on an ocean, which arise through the force of the appearance of inherent existence as existent, even though it is non-existent, and through the force of the adherence to that false appearance as true. As Nāgārjuna says in the eighteenth chapter of his *Fundamental Text Called 'Wisdom'* (*Prajñā-nāma-mūlamadhyamakakārikā*, XVIII. 4–5):

> When the thought of the internal
> And the external as 'I' and 'mine'
> Has perished, grasping ceases
> And through that cessation birth ceases.
>
> When actions and afflictions cease, there is liberation;
> They arise from false conceptions, these arise
> From the elaborations [of false views on inherent
> Existence]; elaborations cease in emptiness.

Inherent existence has never been validly known to exist; therefore, it is impossible for there to be any phenomenon that exists through its own power. Since it is experienced that mere dependent-arisings, which are in fact empty of inherent existence, do cause all forms of help and harm, these are established as existent. Thus, mere dependent-arisings do exist. Therefore, all phenomena exist in the manner of appearing as varieties of dependent-arisings. They appear this way without passing beyond the sphere or condition of having just this nature of being utterly non-inherently existent. Therefore, all phenomena have two entities: one entity that is its superficial mode of appearance and one entity that is its deep mode of being. These two are called respectively conventional truths and ultimate truths.

The Superior (Ārya) Nāgārjuna says in his *Fundamental Text Called 'Wisdom'* (XXIV. 8):

Doctrines taught by the Buddhas
Rely wholly on the two truths,
Conventional and worldly truths
And truths that are ultimate.

Also, the glorious Candrakīrti says in his *Supplement to (Nāgārjuna's) 'Treatise on the Middle Way'* (*Madhyamakāvatāra*, VI. 23)[1]:

[Buddha] said that all phenomena have two entities,
Those found by perceivers of the true and of the false;
Objects of perceivers of the true are realities,
Objects of perceivers of the false are conventional truths.

The divisions of ultimate truths will be briefly explained below. Conventional truths themselves are divided into the real and the unreal just from the point of view of an ordinary worldly consciousness. Candrakīrti says (*Supplement*, VI. 24–25):

Also those which perceive falsities are said to be of two types,
Those with clear senses and those having defective ones.
A consciousness having a defective sense is said to be
Wrong in relation to one with a sense that is sound.

Objects realised by the world and apprehended
By the six non-defective senses are only true
From a worldly point of view, the rest are presented
As unreal only from the viewpoint of the world.

The purpose of knowing thus the presentation of the two truths is as follows. Since it is utterly necessary to be involved with these appearances which bring about varieties of good and bad effects, it is necessary to know the two natures, superficial and deep, of these objects to which we are related. For example, there may be a cunning and deceptive neighbour with whom it is always necessary for us to interact and to whom we have related by way of an estimation of him that accords only with his [pleasant] external appearance. The various losses that we have sustained in this relationship are not due to the fault of our merely having interacted with that man. Rather, the fault lies with our mistaken manner of relating to him. Further, because of not knowing the man's nature, we have not estimated him properly and have thereby been deceived. Therefore, if that man's external appearance and his fundamental nature had both been well known, we would have related to him with a reserve appropriate to his nature and with whatever corresponded to his capacities, and so forth. Had we done this, we would not have sustained any losses.

Similarly, if phenomena had no deep mode of being other than their external or superficial mode of being, and if thus the way they appeared and the way they existed were in agreement, then it would be sufficient to hold that conventional modes of appearance are true just as they appear, and to place confidence in them. However, this is not so. Though phenomena appear as if true, most true, ultimately they are not true. Therefore, phenomena abide in the middle way, not truly or inherently existent and also not utterly non-existent. This view, or way of viewing—the knowledge of such a mode of being, just as it is— is called the view of the middle way.

With respect to this, the way in which there is no inherent existence or self is as follows. Whatever objects appear to us now—forms, sounds and so forth which are cognised by the eyes, ears and so on, or objects cognised by the mind, or objects of experience and so forth—these objects are the bases of negation, in relation to which the object of that negation, inherent existence, is negated. They appear to be inherently existent, or existing as independent entities, or existing objectively. Therefore, all consciousnesses are mistaken except for the wisdom that directly cognises emptiness.

Question: [If all those consciousnesses that are not directly cognising emptiness are mistaken, does this mean that] there are no valid cognisers which could certify the existence of conventionally existent phenomena, such as forms and so on? Or, does this mean that since the criterion for a phenomenon's existing conventionally would have to be its existing for a mistaken, perverse consciousness [rather than its existing for a valid cogniser], it would follow that the non-existence of any phenomenon could not occur [because any phenomenon could be cognised by a mistaken consciousness]?

Answer: It is not contradictory for a consciousness to be mistaken, on the one hand, because objects appear to it as if they inherently existed, and, on the other, for it to be valid, because it is not deceived with respect to its main object. For example, a visual consciousness perceiving a form is indeed a mistaken consciousness because the form appears to it as inherently existent. However, to the extent that it perceives the form as a form and does not *conceive* the form to be inherently existent, it is a valid cogniser. Not only that, but a visual consciousness perceiving a form is also a valid cogniser with respect to the appearance of the form and even with respect to the appearance of the form's seeming to be inherently existent. All dualistic consciousnesses, therefore, are valid direct cognisers with respect to their own objects of perception, because in the expression, 'a consciousness knowing its object', a consciousness refers to a clear knower which is generated in the image of its object through the force of the appearance of its object.

Further, the criterion for a phenomenon's existing conventionally is not merely its existing for a mistaken, perverse consciousness. For example, an appearance of falling hairs manifestly appears to the visual consciousness of someone with cataract. Because his consciousness has been generated in the image of falling hairs, it is a valid, direct cogniser with respect to that object of perception. However, since the falling hairs, which are the basis of such an appearance, are utterly non-existent, the consciousness is deceived with respect to its main object. Thus, because this consciousness of falling hairs is directly contradicted by a consciousness with a valid mode of perception, it is asserted to be a wrong consciousness. How could existing for this mistaken consciousness be the criterion for a phenomenon's existing conventionally?

In short, it is said that though there is no phenomenon that is not posited by the mind, whatever the mind posits is not necessarily existent.

When a phenomenon appears thus to be inherently existent, if the phenomenon existed in the same way as it appeared, then the entity of its inherent existence would necessarily become clearer when its mode of existence was carefully analysed. For example, even in terms of what is widely known in the world, if something is true, it becomes clearer and its foundation more firm the more one analyses it. Therefore, when sought, it must definitely be findable. If, on the contrary, it is false, then when it is analysed and sought, it becomes unclear, and in the end it cannot stand up. Nāgārjuna's *Precious Garland* (*Ratnā-valī*, 52–53) says:

A form seen from a distance
Is seen clearly by those nearby.
If a mirage were water, why
Is water not seen by those nearby?

The way this world is seen
As real by those afar
Is not so seen by those nearby,
[For whom it is] signless like a mirage.

Let us give an example. When it is said and thought that human beings should have happiness, a human who is one who should have happiness appears boldly to our mind as if existing in his own right. To create human happiness, one must achieve the favourable circumstances for physical pleasures such as food, clothing, shelter, medicines and transportation for the body, and the favourable circumstances for mental pleasures such as higher education, respectability, good disposition and tranquility for the mind. It is necessary to create a human's happiness through physical and mental pleasures. That being so, if we search, wondering what the real human is, we find that his body and mind individually are not the human, and there is also no identifying, 'This is the human,' separately from these two.

Similarly, when we have met an acquaintance named 'Lucky', we say, for instance, 'I saw Lucky,' 'Lucky has become old,' or 'Lucky has become fat.' Without analysing or examining those statements, seeing Lucky's body is said to be seeing Lucky; seeing his body weaker is said to be seeing Lucky weaker; and seeing his body larger is said to be seeing Lucky larger. A consciousness that perceives such without analysis is not a wrong consciousness, and these statements also are not false. [However] when analysis is done, a real Lucky himself who is the possessor of the body is not to be seen, and his ageing and becoming fat also cannot stand up to analysis. Further, with respect to the goodness or badness of Lucky's mind, Lucky is designated as a good man or a bad man. But Lucky's mind itself is not Lucky. In short, there is not the slightest part which is Lucky among the mere collection of Lucky's mind and body, his continuum, or individual parts. Therefore, dependent on the mere collection of Lucky's body and mind, we designate 'Lucky'. As Nāgārjuna says in his *Precious Garland* (80):

> The person is not earth, not water,
> Not fire, not wind, not space,
> Not consciousness and not all of them;
> What person is there other than these?

Further, with respect to the statement, 'I saw Lucky's body,' seeing merely the external skin from among the many parts of the body, flesh, skin, bones and so forth, functions as seeing his body. Even if the blood, bones and so forth are not seen, it does not mean that the body is not seen. To see a body it is not necessary to see all of the body; seeing even a small part can function as seeing the body. However, sometimes by the force of general custom, if a certain amount is not seen, it cannot function as a seeing of the body. As above, if the body is divided into its individual parts, legs, arms and so on, a body is not found. Also, the legs and arms can be divided into toes and fingers, the toes and fingers into joints and the joints into upper and lower portions; these can be divided into small parts and even the smallest parts into parts corresponding with the directions. When they are divided in this way, none of these entities are findable. Also, if the smallest particle were directionally partless, that is, if it had no sides, then no matter how many directionally partless particles were collected, they could never be arranged side by side to form a mass.

Furthermore, Lucky is said to be happy or unhappy according to whether his mind is at ease or not. What is this mind which is the basis of this determination? It does not exist as anything physical, it lacks anything tangible, any object can appear to it, and it exists as an entity of mere knowing. Further, it is like this when it is not analysed; but when it is analysed, it is unfindable. When Lucky's mind is happy, the entity of that mind is what is to be analysed. If it is divided into individual moments, there is no mass that is a composite of the many former and later moments. At the time of the later moments, the former moments have ceased; therefore, the former ones have gone and their conscious entity has disappeared. Because the future moments have not yet been produced, they are not existing now. Also, the single present moment is not separate from what has already been produced and what has not yet been produced. Therefore, when it is sought thus, one is unable to establish a present consciousness. When the happy mind, which is the object discussed in 'His mind is happy,' is sought, it is utterly unfindable. In short, happy and unhappy minds and so forth are designated to a mere collection of their own former and future moments. Even the shortest moment is imputed to its own parts; it has the individual parts of a beginning and an end. If a moment were partless, there could be no continuum composed of them.

Similarly, when an external object such as a table appears to the mind, a naturally existent or independent table appears. Let us analyse this table by dividing it into a whole and parts. In general, the table is put as the base of its qualities, and by examining its qualities such as shape, colour, material and size, we can speak of its value, quality and so forth. For example, when we say 'This table is good, but its colour is not good,' there is a table that is the base of the estimation of the quality of its colour. A base of qualities that possesses these qualities does [conventionally] exist, but the qualities and parts individually are not themselves the base of the qualities. Also, after eliminating the qualities and parts, a base of these qualities is not findable. If there is no such base, then since qualities are necessarily established in dependence on a base of qualities and, moreover, since a base of qualities is necessarily established in dependence on qualities, the qualities also will not exist.

Let us illustrate this with the example of a rosary which has one hundred and eight beads. The whole, the one rosary, has one hundred and eight beads as its parts. The parts and the whole are [conventionally] different; yet, when the parts are eliminated, a rosary cannot be found. Because the rosary is one and its parts are many, the rosary is not the same as its parts. When the parts are eliminated, there is no rosary which exists separately; therefore, it is not inherently or fundamentally different from its parts. Because the rosary does not exist separate from its parts, it does not inherently depend on its parts, nor do the parts inherently depend on it. Also, the beads do not inherently belong to the rosary. Similarly, since the shape of the rosary is one of its qualities, this shape is not the rosary. Also, the collection of the beads and the string is the basis in dependence on which the rosary is imputed; therefore, it is not the rosary. If it is sought in this way, a rosary is unfindable as any of the seven extremes. Further, if the individual beads are sought as above, that is, as one with their parts, or different from their parts and so forth, they are unfindable as well. Furthermore, since forests, armies, continents, and countries are imputed to aggregations of many parts, when each is analysed as to whether it is this or not that, it is utterly unfindable.

Further, it is extremely clear that good and bad, tall and short, big and small, enemy and friend, father and son and so forth are all imputations of the one based on the other. Also earth, water, fire, wind and so on are each imputed in dependence on their parts. Space is imputed in dependence on its parts, which pervade the directions. Also, Buddhas and sentient beings, cyclic existence and nirvāṇa and so forth are only just imputed in dependence on their parts and their bases of imputation.

Just as it is widely known that, 'An effect is produced from causes,' so production does exist [conventionally]. However, let us analyse the meaning of production. If effects were produced causelessly, they would either always be produced or would never be produced. If they were produced from themselves, it would be purposeless for what has already attained its own entity to be produced again; and if what had already been produced is produced again, then there is the consequent fallacy that its reproduction would be endless. If effects were produced from entities other than themselves, they would be produced from everything, both from what are considered conventionally to be their causes and from what are not [since both are equally other]. Or, it would be contradictory for effects to depend on causes [for, being totally separate, they could not be inter-related]. Production from both self and others is not possible either [because of the faults in both these positions demonstrated separately above]. Thus, if the meaning of the designation 'production' is sought, production is not capable of being established. As the Superior Nāgārjuna says in his *Fundamental Text Called 'Wisdom'* (I. 1):

> There is never production
> Anywhere of any phenomenon
> From itself, from others,
> From both, or without cause.

Though it is widely known [and conventionally correct] that causes do produce effects, let us analyse these effects. If the produced effect inherently existed, how could it be correct for what already exists to be produced newly? For, causes are not needed to create it anew. In general, causes conventionally do newly create that which has not been produced or which is non-existent at the time of its causes. However, if the non-produced were inherently true as non-produced, it would be no different from being utterly non-existent; therefore, how could it be fit for production by causes? As Nāgārjuna says in his *Seventy Stanzas on Emptiness* (*Śūnyatāsaptati*):

> Because it exists, the existent is not produced;
> Because it does not exist, the non-existent is not produced.

In short, once the existence of something is necessarily dependent on causes and conditions and on others, then it is contradictory for it to exist independently. For, independence and dependence on others are contradictory. The *Questions of the King of Nāgas, Anavatapta, Sūtra* (*Anavataptanāgarāja-paripṛcchā*) says:

> That which is produced from causes is not [inherently] produced,
> It does not have an inherent nature of production.
> That which depends on causes is said to be
> Empty; he who knows emptiness is aware.

Nāgārjuna's *Fundamental Text Called 'Wisdom'* (XXIV. 19) says:

> Because there are no phenomena
> Which are not dependent-arisings,
> There are no phenomena
> Which are not empty.

Āryadeva says in his *Four Hundred* (*Catuḥṡataka*, XIV. 23):

> That which has dependent-arising
> Cannot be self-powered; since all these
> Lack independence there can be
> No self [no inherent existence].

If phenomena were not empty of a fundamental basis or of inherent existence, it would be utterly impossible for the varieties of phenomena to be transformed in dependence on causes. If they existed by way of their own fundamental basis, then no matter what type of entity they were, good, bad and so on, how could they be changed? If a good fruit tree, for instance, were inherently existent by way of its own entity or its own inner basis, how would it be true that it could become bare and ugly? If the present mode of appearance of these things to our minds were their own inner mode of being, how could we be deceived? Even in the ordinary world many discrepancies are well known between what appears and what actually is. Therefore, although beginninglessly everything has appeared as if it were inherently existent to the mind that is contaminated with the errors of ignorance, if those objects were indeed inherently existent, their inner basis would be just as they appear. In that case, when the consciousness searching for the inner basis of a phenomenon performed analysis, that inner basis would definitely become clearer. Where does the fault lie, that when sought, phenomena are not found and seemingly disappear?

Further, if things inherently existed, it would be as Candra-kīrti says in his *Supplement* (VI. 34–36)[2]:

> If the inherent existence [of phenomena] depended [on causes, the yogī
> Realising emptiness], by denying that, would be destroying phenomena;
> Therefore, [seeing] emptiness would be a cause which destroys phenomena, but since
> This is not reasonable, phenomena do not [inherently exist].

> When these phenomena are analysed, they are not found
> To abide as other than phenomena with the nature
> Of reality [having no inherently existent production or cessation];
> Therefore, worldly conventional truths are not to be analysed.

> When reality [is analysed] production
> From self and other is not admissible,
> Through the same reasoning [inherently existent production] also is not admissible
> Conventionally; how then could your [inherently existent] production be [established]?

Thus, Candrakīrti is saying that if phenomena existed naturally or inherently, it would follow that a Superior's meditative equipoise realising emptiness would cause the destruction of these phenomena. Also, it would follow that conventional truths would be able to stand up to a reasoned analysis. Further, it would follow that production would not be ultimately refuted, and that many sūtras which teach that phenomena are empty of themselves in the sense that they are empty of their own natural inherent existence would be wrong. For instance, a Mother Sūtra, the *Twenty-Five Thousand Stanza Perfection of Wisdom Sūtra* (*Pañcaviṃśatisāhasrikāprajñāpāramitā*) says, 'With respect to this, Śāriputra, when a Bodhisattva, a great being, practises the perfection of wisdom, he does not see a Bodhisattva as real. . . . Why? Śāriputra, it is like this: a Bodhisattva is empty of being an inherently existent Bodhisattva. A Bodhisattva's name also is empty of being a Bodhisattva's name. Why? That is their nature. It is like this: it is not that a form is empty on account of emptiness; emptiness is not separate from a form. A form itself is [that which is] empty; just [that which is] empty is also the form.' Further, the *Kāśyapa Chapter* in the *Pile of Jewels Sūtra* (*Ratnakūṭa*) says, 'Phenomena are not made empty by emptiness, the phenomena themselves are empty.' Therefore, all phenomena lack inherent existence or their own basic foundation.

Question: If a real man and a dream man, a form and a reflection, a real thing and a picture are the same in that they are not found when sought, would it not follow that there would be no differences among them? There would be no differences as to their truth, falsity and so forth. Thus, what would be the use of searching into the view of emptiness? For, the searcher and the view itself would be none other than non-existent.

Answer: This touches on a difficult point. There is a great danger that because of this subtle point those of immature intelligence might fall to a view of nihilism. Therefore, to avoid that, some who were skilled in means, the Svātantrika-Mādhyamika Bhāvaviveka and his spiritual sons [Jñānagarbha, Śāntarakṣita, Kamalaśīla, etc.], used reasoning to refute that phenomena exist from the point of view of their own particular mode of subsistence and without being established through their appearance to a faultless consciousness. However, they asserted natural or inherent existence conventionally. For those whose minds could not cope even with this type of truthlessness, the Cittamātrin teachers, Vasubandhu and so forth, used reasoning to refute external objects, yet asserted that the mind does truly exist. For those who could not be vessels of a teaching of the selflessness of phenomena, the proponents of truly existing external objects--the Vaibhāṣikas and Sautrāntikas—asserted in the place of emptiness a mere selflessness, which is the person's non-existence as a substantial or self-sufficient entity. The non-Buddhists could not even assert the mere selflessness of persons, and from that, therefore, they derive the necessity of asserting a permanent, partless, independent person.

Question: If it is asserted that phenomena do not exist by reason of their not being found when the object imputed is sought, that contradicts what is widely known in the world; for it goes against obvious experience. Our own experience affirms the existence of these phenomena which are all included in the terms 'environments' and 'beings'. Our own experience affirms as well the fact that varieties of help, harm, pleasure and pain are produced. Thus, what is the meaning of not being able to find such things as self and other, environments and beings, when we seek these varieties of definitely existent phenomena?

Answer: The *Twenty-Five Thousand Stanza Perfection of Wisdom Sūtra* says, 'It is thus: this "Bodhisattva" is only a name; this "perfection of wisdom" is only a name; these "forms", "feelings", "discriminations", "compositional factors", and "consciousnesses" are only names. It is thus: forms are like illusions. Feelings, discriminations, compositional factors and consciousnesses are like illusions. Illusions also are only names; they do not abide in places; they do not abide in the directions. . . . Why? It is thus: names are fabricated and imputed to the individual phenomena, names are adventitiously designated. They are all designations. When a Bodhisattva, a great being, practices the perfection of wisdom, he does not view names as real. Because he does not view them as real, he does not adhere to them. Further, O Śāriputra, when a Bodhisattva, a great being, practises the perfection of wisdom, he thinks thus: this "Bodhisattva" is only a name; this "enlightenment" is only a name; this "perfection of wisdom" is only a name; these "forms" are only names; these "feelings", "discriminations", "compositional factors" and "consciousnesses" are only names. Sāriputra, it is thus: "I" for example is designated, but the "I" is unapprehendable.' In many sūtras and treatises phenomena are all said to be only names. When imputed objects are sought, they are utterly not there in any objective way. This is a sign that all phenomena are not objectively existent and are only established as existing through subjective designations and thoughts. Existing merely in this way functions as existing.

Let us explain this further in fine detail. For something to exist conventionally, it must satisfy three criteria:

1 The object must be generally well known to a conventional consciousness. Yet, if merely being well known were sufficient [to establish the conventional existence of an object], then even the commonly cited 'son of a barren woman' would exist. Therefore, for any object to exist conventionally,

2 It must not be possible for a conventional valid cogniser to contradict it. Yet, since a conventional valid cogniser cannot refute inherent existence [which otherwise would exist conventionally by merely the above two criteria],

3 It must not be possible for a reasoning that analyses the ultimate to refute it either.

Therefore, an entity existing objectively without existing merely through the force of subjective designations is the measure or meaning of what is negated; it is that of which phenomena are empty in the expression 'emptiness'. It is also called 'self' or 'object negated by reasoning'. Since it is utterly not known validly to exist, a consciousness that adheres to it as existent is called an ignorant consciousness. In general, there are many types of mere ignorance; however, that which is being explained here is the ignorance that is the root of cyclic existence, the opposite of the wisdom that cognises selflessness. Nāgārjuna's *Seventy Stanzas on Emptiness* says:

> The thought that phenomena produced
> From causes and conditions are real
> Was called ignorance by the Teacher;
> From it the twelve branches[3] arise.

A mere non-existence of the self which is the object of negation, that is, the mere non-existence of an inherent existence as apprehended by such an ignorant consciousness, is called a selflessness, a truthlessness and an emptiness. Just this is the deep mode of subsistence or final mode of being of all phenomena; therefore, it is called an ultimate truth. A consciousness that cognises it is called a consciousness cognising an emptiness.

Question: Since emptinesses are ultimate truths, do emptinesses themselves exist?

Answer: An emptiness is the way of being, or mode of existence, of the phenomenon qualified by it. Therefore, if the phenomenon qualified by an emptiness does not exist, there is no emptiness of it. The empty nature of a phenomenon is established in relation to that phenomenon which is qualified by this empty nature, and a phenomenon qualified by an empty nature is established in relation to its empty nature. Just as when a phenomenon qualified by an empty nature is analysed it is not found, so too when this phenomenon's empty nature itself is analysed, it is unfindable as well. Therefore, when we seek the object designated as 'an empty nature', this empty nature is also not found. It merely exists through the force of subjective designation done without analysis. Thus it does not inherently exist. The thirteenth chapter of Nāgārjuna's *Fundamental Text Called 'Wisdom'* (XIII. 7–8) says:

> If anything non-empty existed, then
> Something empty would also exist;

> If the non-empty does not exist
> At all, how could the empty do so?

> The Conquerors said that emptiness
> Is the remover of all [bad] views;
> Those who view emptiness [as inherently existent]
> Were said to be incurable.

Also, Nāgārjuna's *Praise of the Supramundane* (*Lokātītastava*) says:

> Since the ambrosia of emptiness is taught
> For the sake of forsaking all misconceptions,
> He who adheres to it [as inherently existent]
> Is strongly berated by you [the Buddha].

Therefore, when a tree, for instance, is analysed, the tree is not found, but its mode of being or emptiness is found. Then, when that emptiness is analysed, that emptiness also is not found, but the emptiness of that emptiness is found. This is called an emptiness of an emptiness. Thus, a tree is a conventional truth, and its mode of being is an ultimate truth. Further, when that ultimate truth becomes the basis of analysis and when its mode of being is posited, then that ultimate truth becomes the basis of qualification in relation to the quality that is its mode of being. Thus, there is even an explanation that in these circumstances an emptiness can be viewed as a conventional truth.

Though there are no essential differences among emptinesses, it is said that emptinesses are divided into twenty, eighteen, sixteen, or four types in terms of the bases qualified by emptiness. Briefly, all are included within these two categories: selflessness of persons and selflessness of other phenomena.

Question: How does an emptiness appear to a mind when it ascertains an emptiness?

Answer: If one has a mistaken view of an emptiness, equating it with a vacuity which is a nothingness, this is not the ascertainment of an emptiness. Or, even if one has developed a proper understanding of an emptiness as merely a lack of inherent existence, still, when the vacuity which is a lack of inherent existence appears, one may subsequently lose sight of the original understanding. This vacuity then becomes a mere nothingness with the original understanding of the negation of inherent existence being lost completely. Therefore, this is not the ascertainment of an emptiness either. Also, even if the meaning of an emptiness has been ascertained, but the thought, 'This is an emptiness,' appears, then one is apprehending the existence of an emptiness which is a positive thing. Therefore, that consciousness then becomes a conventional valid cogniser and not the ascertainment of an emptiness. The *Condensed Perfection of Wisdom Sūtra* (*Sañcayagāthā-prajñāpāramitā*) says, 'Even if a Bodhisattva realises, "These aggregates are empty," he is acting on signs of conventionalities and does not have faith in the state of non-production.'

Further, 'an emptiness' is a negative [an absence] which must be ascertained through the mere elimination of the object of negation, that is, inherent existence. Negatives are of two types: affirming negatives in which some other positive phenomenon is implied in place of the object of negation, and non-affirming negatives in which no other positive phenomenon is implied in place of the object of negation. An emptiness is an instance of the latter; therefore, a consciousness cognising an emptiness necessarily ascertains the mere negative or absence of the object of negation. What appears to the mind is a clear vacuity accompanied by the mere thought, 'These concrete things as they now appear to our minds do not exist at all.' The mere lack of inherent existence or mere truthlessness which is the referent object of this consciousness is an emptiness; therefore, such a mind ascertains an emptiness. Śāntideva's *Engaging in the Bodhisattva Deeds* (IX. 34–35)[4] says:

When with the thought 'it does not exist' the thing analysed
Is not apprehended [as inherently existent],
How could there stand before the mind an [inherently existent]
   non-thing lacking
A base [that is, an inherently existent emptiness without the
   object it qualifies]?

When [inherently existent] things
And non-things do not stand before the mind,
Since there is nothing else [inherently existent],
Then with the intended objects [of the conception
Of inherent existence] being non-existent, elaborations
[Of duality and inherent existence] are extinguished.

If an emptiness were not a non-affirming negative but were
either an affirming negative implying another phenomenon or
a positive phenomenon itself, then a consciousness cognising
it would have apprehension [of an inherent existence] or
would be involved with signs [of conventionalities]. Thus,
the possibility of generating a conceiver of inherent existence
would not be eliminated. In that case, the wisdom cognising
emptiness would not be the antidote of all conceptions of
inherent existence and would be incapable of eliminating the
obstructions to enlightenment. Thinking of this, Śāntideva
says in his *Engaging in the Bodhisattva Deeds* (IX. 110–111)[5]:

[*Question*]

When the analyser analysing [whether phenomena inherently
   exist]
Analyses [and determines that they are empty of inherent
   existence],
Because the analyser also is to be analysed,
Would it not then be endless?

[*Answer*]

> If the objects of analysis [all phenomena in general]
> Have been analysed [and determined not to exist inherently],
> Then [for that mind] no [further inherently existent] basis
>   [requiring more analysis] exists.
> Because the bases [which are the phenomena qualified by
>   emptiness] do not inherently exist,
> [An object of negation], inherent existence and its negative
> Are not inherently produced, that too is called [the natural]
>   nirvāṇa.[6]

Thus, viewing a base—self, other, and so forth—we ascertain the meaning of its being essentially or naturally at peace, free of inherent existence. If we become familiar with this, the objects viewed—self, other, and so forth—appear as illusion-like or dream-like falsities which, although not inherently existent, appear to be so.

Question: What is the imprint or benefit of such an ascertainment of an emptiness?

Answer: Nāgārjuna's *Fundamental Text Called 'Wisdom'* (XXIV. 18) says:

> That which is dependent-arising
> We explain as emptiness.
> This is dependent imputation;
> Just this is the middle path.

Thus, we understand the natural lack of inherent existence to be the meaning of dependent-arising and understand dependent-arising to be the meaning of the natural lack of inherent existence. Then, we ascertain that emptiness and dependent-arising accompany each other. Through the force of this ascertainment, conventional valid cognisers properly engage in that which is to be adopted and cease doing that which is to be discarded within the context of mere nominal existence. Perverse consciousnesses such as desire, hatred and so forth, generated through the force of adhering to objective existence or non-nominal existence, become gradually weaker and can finally be abandoned.

Let us explain this a little. If the actual experience of the view of emptiness has arisen, we can identify within our experience that whatever objects presently appear to our consciousnesses [eye, ear and so on], they all seem to be inherently existent. We can then know with certainty how the conceiver of inherent existence is generated, and how—at the time of strong attention to these objects—it adheres to the way they appear, and posits them to be true. We will then further know that whatever afflictions are produced, such as desire, hatred, and so forth, a conceiver of inherent existence is acting as their basic cause. Moreover, we will ascertain clearly that this conceiver of inherent existence is a perverse consciousness that is mistaken with respect to its referent object. We will know with certainty how the mode of apprehension of this consciousness lacks a valid foundation. We will also know that its opposite, a consciousness which perceives a selflessness, is a non-perverse consciousness and that its mode of apprehension has the support of valid cognition.

Thus, the glorious Dharmakīrti says in his *Commentary on (Dignāga's) 'Compendium on Valid Cognisers'* (*Pramāṇavārttika*, Chapter I)[7]:

> An ascertaining mind and a falsely superimposing mind
> Are entities of eradicator and that which is eradicated.

And (Chapter I):

> All [defects such as desires] have as their antidote [the wisdom of selflessness]
> In that their decrease and increase depend [on the increase and decrease of that wisdom].
> So through familiarity the mind assumes the nature of
> That wisdom—thus in time the contaminations are extinguished.

A conceiver of inherent existence and a consciousness that has a contradictory mode of apprehension are respectively the eradicated and eradicator. Therefore, it is natural that if one becomes stronger, the other will become weaker. Nāgārjuna's *Praise of the Element of Superior Qualities* (*Dharmadhātustotra*) says:

> When a metal garment which has become stained with
> Contaminations and is to be cleansed by fire,
> Is put in fire, its stains
> Are burned but it is not,
>
> So, with regard to the mind of clear light
> Which has the stains of desire and so forth,
> Its stains are burned by the fire of wisdom
> But its nature, clear light, is not.

The Conqueror Maitreya's *Sublime Science* (*Uttaratantra*)[8] says:

> Because the bodies of a perfect Buddha are emanated [to all
>   sentient beings], because reality
> Is not differentiated [since it is the final nature of both Buddhas
>   and sentient beings],
> And because [sentient beings] have the [natural and develop-
>   mental] lineages [suitable
> To develop into a Truth Body and a Form Body],
> Then all embodied beings have the Buddha Nature.

Thus, not only is the ultimate nature of the mind unpolluted by contaminations, but also the conventional nature of the mind, that is, its mere clear knowing, is unpolluted by contaminations as well. Therefore, the mind can become either better or worse, and it is suitable to be transformed. However, no matter how much one cultivates the bad consciousnesses that provide a support for the conception of inherent existence, they cannot be cultivated limitlessly. Cultivation of the good consciousnesses, on the other hand, which are opposite to those and which have the support of valid cognition, can be increased limitlessly. On the basis of this reason, we can ascertain that the stains on the mind can be removed. Thus, the final nature of a mind that has removed its stains so that they will never be generated again is liberation. Therefore, we can become certain that liberation is attainable. Not only that, but just as the contaminations of the afflictions are removable, so are their predispositions as well. Therefore, we can be certain that the final nature of the mind with all the contaminations of the afflictions and their predispositions removed is attainable. This is called a non-abiding nirvāṇa or a Body of Truth. Thereby it is generally established that liberation and omniscience exist.

Nāgārjuna's *Fundamental Text Called 'Wisdom'* (I. Invocation) says:

> I bow down to the perfect Buddha,
> The best of teachers, who propounded
> That what dependently arises
> Has no cessation, no production,
> No annihilation, no permanence, no coming,
> No going, no difference, no sameness,
> Is free of the elaborations [of inherent
> Existence and of duality] and is at peace.

Thus Buddha, the Blessed One, from his own insight taught this dependent-arising as his slogan—showing that because phenomena are dependent-arisings, they have a nature of emptiness, free of the eight extremes of cessation and so forth. If Buddha is thus seen as a reliable being who without error taught definite goodness [liberation and omniscience] along with its means, one will consequently see that the Blessed One was not mistaken even with respect to teaching high status [the pleasures of lives as men and gods] along with its means.

The glorious Dharmakīrti says in his *Commentary on (Dignāga's) 'Compendium on Valid Cognisers'* (Chapter I)[9]:

> Because [it is established by common inference that Buddha's word] is not mistaken with regard to the principal meaning [the four truths],
> [Due to similarity, Buddha's word] can be inferred [to be not mistaken] with regard to other [extremely obscure subjects as well].

Also, Āryadeva's *Four Hundred* (Chapter XII)[10] says:

> Whoever has generated doubt
> Towards what is not obvious in Buddha's word
> Will believe that only Buddha [is omniscient]
> Based on [his profound teaching of] emptiness.

In brief, through coming to know the Conqueror's scriptures as well as their commentaries, which are all aimed at the achievement of high status and definite goodness, we will attain faith in them. Thereby, induced by valid cognition, we will generate from our hearts faith and respect for the teacher of these scriptures, the Blessed Buddha, and for his followers, the great masters of India. Similarly, we will be able also to generate firm, unchangable faith and respect for the spiritual guides who presently teach us the paths without error and for the Spiritual Community who are our friends abiding properly on the paths on which the Teacher himself travelled. The master Candrakīrti says in his *Seventy Stanzas on the Three Refuges (Triśaraṇasaptati)*[11]:

> The Buddha, his Doctrine and the Supreme Community
> Are the refuges of those wishing liberation.

Thus, we will easily generate certainty that the Three Refuges are the sole source of refuge for those wishing liberation. Those bothered by suffering will go to the Three Excellences for refuge and will generate a firm, indestructible attitude of wishing for liberation, thinking, 'If I could only attain liberation!' Similarly, having understood the suffering condition of all other sentient beings from our own experience of suffering, we will generate the wish to establish them as well in liberation, that is, in emancipation from suffering, and in omniscience. For the sake of accomplishing this, an extremely steady and very powerful aspiration to enlightenment, wishing to attain enlightenment ourselves, will be produced, and the ability to generate this attitude will arise.

If our motivation is that of a Hīnayānist, working only for our own release from cyclic existence, our progress is as follows. First, we establish as our foundation any of the forms of ethics for householders or monks. Then with this foundation as our base, when we are on the path of accumulation, we familiarise ourselves again and again with the subtle, deep and very meaningful view of emptiness explained above through hearing and thinking about it. Thereby, our viewing consciousness gradually develops into the wisdom which arises from meditation and which is the union of calm abiding and special insight cognising an emptiness conceptually. In this way, the path of preparation is attained. Then, gradually we attain the path of seeing, a true path, a jewel of doctrine, perceiving emptiness directly. [Thus paths in this context are states of consciousness leading to a nirvāṇa, and] through the path of seeing acting as an antidote, we begin to attain true cessations of suffering. These true cessations are states of having utterly abandoned forever both true sources of suffering, such as intellectually acquired conceptions of inherent existence, as well as true sufferings, such as rebirths in bad migrations. That which is abandoned in both cases follows a progression of increasing refinement. Thus, through the path of meditation, which is a further familiarisation with the truth, i.e., emptiness, already seen, we attain step by step the true cessations, which are states of having utterly abandoned forever the innate afflictions, again beginning with the gross ones. Finally, when we attain liberation, which is the state of having abandoned the subtlest of the small afflictions together with their seeds, the travelling of our own path [as a Hīnayānist] has finished. Thus is realised the stage of no more learning, a position reached in the Hīnayāna by a Foe Destroyer [or *arhan*, the chief enemy being the conception of inherent existence].

When our motivation is to attain highest enlightenment for the sake of all sentient beings, the wisdoms of hearing, thinking, and meditating, directed towards the meaning of emptiness, are generated in such a way that they are accompanied by the skilful means of the perfections [giving, ethics, patience, effort, concentration, and wisdom], which arise from this Mahāyāna motivation. The view becomes more and more profound, and when emptiness is cognised directly, the path of seeing, and simultaneously the wisdom of the first stage of the Mahāyāna, are both attained. The first of the accumulations of wisdom and merit, which takes one countless aeon [begun on the path of accumulation], is thus completed. As was previously explained, we then begin to realise the true cessations, which are states of having utterly abandoned forever the intellectually acquired conceptions of inherent existence and so on. Then, during the seven impure Bodhisattva stages, the accumulations of merit and wisdom are amassed over a second countless aeon. During the three pure stages we begin the gradual abandonment of the obstructions to simultaneous cognition of all objects of knowledge. These obstructions are the predispositions that have been established by the conception of inherent existence and the subtle bad habits produced by them. When the third accumulation over a countless aeon is completed, a Body of Truth, a true cessation, which is the state of having utterly abandoned forever all types of defects, is attained. The Three Bodies of Truth, Complete Enjoyment, and Emanation are simultaneously manifested, and the position of Buddhahood, which is the perfection of wisdom, love, and power, is realised.

Moreover, if we have trained our mental continuum well by means of:

1 the thought definitely to leave cyclic existence,
2 the altruistic aspiration to highest enlightenment, and
3 the correct view of emptiness,

and, in addition, have the fortune of having completed well
the causal collections of both merit and wisdom [then we are
qualified to enter the tantric path]. If from among the quick
paths of Secret Mantra we advance through any of the paths
of the three lower tantras, we will become enlightened more
quickly [than had we followed the sūtra paths alone]. Enlightenment is speedily attained through the power of special
means for achieving a Form Body and through the quick
achievement of the yoga of the union of calm abiding and
special insight, and so forth. Further, on the path of the fourth
and highest tantra we learn, in addition to the former practices,
to differentiate the coarse, subtle, and extremely subtle winds
[energies] and consciousnesses. The extremely subtle mental
consciousness itself is generated into the entity of a path
consciousness, and through cultivating it, the consciousness
cognising emptiness becomes extremely powerful. Thus, the
highest tantra has the distinguishing feature of making the
abandonment of obstructions extremely swift.

Let us speak briefly about how to internalise the view of
emptiness. Meditation on the view of emptiness is done for the
sake of abandoning obstructions; therefore, a vast collection
of merit is needed. Further, to amass such through the rite of
the seven branches encompasses much and has great purpose.
The seven branches are prostrating, offering, revealing our
own faults, admiring our own and others' virtues, petitioning
the Buddhas to teach, entreating the Buddhas to remain in the
world, and dedicating the merit of such to all sentient beings.
With regard to the field for amassing the collection of merit,
it is permissible to do whatever suits our own inclinations,
either directing our mind towards the actual Three Excellences
in general or towards any particular object of refuge that is

visualised in front of ourselves. [For this see the *Precious Garland*, 466–85 in volume 2 of this series.]

Then, after we petition the refuges for help in generating the view of emptiness in our continuum, the way to conduct the actual meditation session is as follows. If initially we meditate on the selflessness of the person, it is said to be easier for meditation, because the subject [is continually present]. Therefore, we should ascertain well how the meditator appears to our mind in the thought, 'Now I am meditating on the view of emptiness.' We should ascertain well how the 'I' appears to the mind when the 'I' experiences pleasure or pain. We should also ascertain well the mode of the adherence to the 'I'. Based on that, we should analyse the way the 'I' exists as was explained above. Gradually our understanding and experience of the view of emptiness becomes more profound, and when we engage in analysis at that point, the thought will arise, 'The independent mode of appearance of the "I", such as previously appeared, is utterly non-existent.' At that time, we should set our mind single-pointedly for a period of time on just that clear vacuity which is the mere negative of the object of negation and then perform stabilising meditation without analysis. If our mind's mode of apprehension of this clear vacuity of the negation loosens slightly [and this vacuity starts to become a mere nothingness], then we should again perform analytical meditation on the 'I' as before. Alternately sustaining analytical and stabilising meditation thus serves as a means of transforming the mind.

If through having analysed the 'I' a little understanding of emptiness arises, we should then analyse the mental and physical aggregates in dependence on which the 'I' is imputed. It is very important to analyse well the aggregates of forms, feelings, discriminations, compositional factors, and consciousnesses in general and the aggregate of consciousnesses in particular. Further, it is in general difficult to identify even the conventional mode of being of the mind. Once the conventional nature of the mind—the mere clear knower—has been identified, then, through analysing its nature, finally we will gradually be able to identify the ultimate nature of the mind. If that is done, there is great progress unlike anything else.

At the beginning we should meditate for half an hour. When we rise from the session and various good and bad objects appear, benefit and harm are manifestly experienced. Therefore, we should develop as much as we can the realisation that these phenomena do not exist objectively and are mere dependent-arisings of appearances, like illusions [in that they only seem to be inherently existent].

We should meditate in this way in four formal sessions: at sunrise, in the morning, afternoon, and evening. Or, if possible, we should meditate in six or eight or more sessions, scheduling them at equal intervals throughout the day and night. If this is not possible, we should meditate in only two sessions, in the morning and the evening. When our understanding and experience of the view of emptiness become a little stronger, ascertainment of the view will arise spontaneously during all activities, when we are going, wandering, sleeping, or staying. Also, since without a calm abiding directed toward an emptiness there is no chance for generating a special insight that cognises an emptiness, it is definitely necessary to seek a calm abiding. Therefore, we should learn its methods from other books.

If we do not wish merely to know intellectually about the view of emptiness, but rather wish to experience it ourselves in our own continuum, we should build a firm foundation for this through what has been explained above. Then, according to our mental ability we should hear and consider both the sūtras and treatises which teach the profound view of emptiness as well as the good explanations of them by the experienced Tibetan scholars in their commentaries. Together with this, we should learn to make our own ways of generating experience of emptiness accord with the precepts of an experienced wise man.

> Through the collections of virtues arising from my effort here
> May all sentient beings wishing happiness, myself and others,
> Attain the eye which sees reality, free of extremes,
> And proceed to the land of enlightenment.

This has been written for the sake of helping in general those with burgeoning intellect in the East and West and in particular those who, though they wish to know the very profound and subtle meaning of emptiness or selflessness, either do not have the opportunity to study the great Mādhyamika books or cannot read and understand the treatises existing in the Tibetan language. Thus, it has been written mainly with the intent of easy comprehension and for the sake of easy translation into other languages. May this which has been written by the Buddhist monk, Tenzin Gyatso, bring virtuous goodness.

Notes

Except where noted, all editions are those in the rNam-rgyal Grva-tshang Library in Dharamsala. For the titles of the commentaries see the Bibliography.

1 The *Fundamental Text Called 'Wisdom'* and the *Treatise on the Middle Way* are the same book. This and the next quote are translated in accordance with Tsong-ka-pa's commentary.

2 The parenthetical additions are from Tsong-ka-pa's commentary: Tokyo-Kyoto ed., vol 154 49-1-1 through 51-1-7.

3 Ignorance, action, consciousness, name and form, six sources, contact, feeling, attachment, grasping, existence, birth, and ageing and death.

4 Parenthetical additions are from Gyel-tsap's (rGyal-tshab) commentary, 127a.2 through 127a.5.

5 Parenthetical additions are from Gyel-tsap's commentary, 145a.1 through 145b.2.

6 According to Gyel-tsap: That absence of inherent existence is said to be the natural nirvāṇa of all phenomena. Or, another meaning of the line, also according to Gyel-tsap: Through realising and meditating on the meaning of non-inherent existence it is said that nirvāṇa is attained.

7 Parenthetical additions to the second quote are from Kay-drup's (mKhas-grub) commentary, 134b.3-4.

8 Parenthetical additions are from Gyel-tsap's commentary, 73b.5 through 74a.2.

9 Parenthetical additions are from Kay-drup's commentary, 135b.6-7.

10 Parenthetical additions are from Gyel-tsap's commentary, 90b.3 through 91a.3.

11 Page 279b.4, volume khi of the sNar-thang bsTan-'gyur in the Library of Tibetan Works and Archives, Dharamsala.

Bibliography

The number of the texts and volumes in the Suzuki Research Foundation publication of the Peking edition are given after the Sanskrit and Tibetan titles.

I TEXTS QUOTED BY THE AUTHOR

Commentary on (Dignāga's) 'Compendium on Valid Cognisers' by Dharma-kīrti
Pramāṇavārttika
Tshad ma rnam 'grel
(P5709, vol 130)

Condensed Perfection of Wisdom Sūtra by Buddha
Sañcayagāthā-prajñāpāramitā-sūtra
Shes rab kyi pha rol tu phyin pa sdud pa tshigs su bcad pa
(P735, vol 21)

Engaging in the Bodhisattva Deeds by Śāntideva
Bodhicaryāvatāra
Byang chub sems dpa'i spyod pa la 'jug pa
(P5272, vol 99)

Four Hundred or *Treatise of Four Hundred Stanzas* by Āryadeva
Catuḥśatakaśāstrakārikā
bsTan bcos bzhi brgya pa zhes bya ba'i tshig le'ur byas pa
(P5246, vol 95)

Fundamental Text Called 'Wisdom' or *Fundamental Stanzas on the Middle Way Called 'Wisdom'* by Nāgārjuna
Prajñā-nāma-mūlamadhyamakakārikā
dBu ma rtsa ba'i tshig le'ur byas pa shes rab ces bya ba
(P5224, vol 95)

Hundred Thousand Stanza Perfection of Wisdom Sūtra by Buddha
Śatasāhasrikā-prajñāpāramitā-sūtra
Shes rab kyi pha rol tu phyin pa stong phrag brgya pa
(P730, vol 12–18)

Kāśyapa Chapter in the *Pile of Jewels Sūtra* by Buddha
Kāśyapaparivarta-sūtra [in the] Ratnakūṭa-sūtra
'Od srung gi le'u'i mdo [in the] dKon mchog brtseg pa'i mdo
(P760–43, vol 24)

91

Ornament of the Mahāyāna Sūtras by Maitreya
Mahāyānasūtrālamkāra
Theg pa chen po'i mdo sde'i rgyan
(P5521, vol 108)

Praise of the Element of Superior Qualities by Nāgārjuna
Dharmadhātustotra
Chos kyi dbyings su bstod pa
(P2010, vol 46)

Praise of the Supramundane by Nāgārjuna
Lokātītastava
'Jig rten las 'das par bstod pa
(P2012, vol 46)

Precious Garland of Advice for the King by Nāgārjuna
Rājaparikathāratnāvalī
rGyal po la gtam bya ba rin po che'i phreng ba
(P5658, vol 129)

Questions of the King of Nāgas, Anavatapta, Sūtra by Buddha
Anavataptanāgarājaparipṛcchā-sūtra
Klu'i rgyal po ma dros pas zhus pa'i mdo
(P823, vol 33)

Seventy Stanzas on Emptiness by Nāgārjuna
Śūnyatāsaptatikārikā
sTong pa nyid bdun cu pa'i tshig le'ur byas pa
(P5227, vol 95)

Seventy Stanzas on the Three Refuges by Candrakīrti
Triśaraṇasaptati
gSum la skyabs su 'gro ba bdun cu pa
(P5366, vol 103)

Sublime Science or *Mahāyāna Treatise on the Sublime Science* by Maitreya
Mahāyānottaratantraśāstra
Theg pa chen po rgyud bla ma'i bstan bcos
(P5525, vol. 108)

Supplement to (Nāgārjuna's) 'Treatise on the Middle Way' by Candrakīrti
Madhyamakāvatāra
dBu ma la 'jug pa
(P5262, vol 98)

Sūtra on the Four Truths by Buddha
Catuḥsatya-sūtra
bDen pa bzhi'i mdo
(P982, vol 39)

92

Twenty-Five Thousand Stanza Perfection of Wisdom Sūtra by Buddha
Pañcaviṃśatisāhasrikā-prajñāpāramitā-sūtra
Shes rab kyi pha rol tu phyin pa stong phrag nyi shu lnga pa
(P731, vol 18–19)
Unravelling of the Thought Sūtra by Buddha
Saṃdhinirmocana-sūtra
dGongs pa nges par 'grel pa'i mdo
P774, vol 29)

II COMMENTARIES CITED BY THE TRANSLATORS

Brilliant Illumination of the Thought, An Explanation of (Candrakīrti's)
Treatise 'Supplement to (Nāgārjuna's) "Fundamental Treatise on the
Middle Way"' by Tsong-ka-pa (Tsong-kha-pa)
bsTan bcos chen po dbu ma la 'jug pa'i rnam bshad dgongs pa rab gsal
(P6143, vol 154)
Commentary on (Maitreya's) 'Mahāyāna Treatise on the Sublime Science'
by Gyel-tsap (rGyal-tshab)
Theg pa chen po rgyud bla ma'i ṭīkā
Entrance of the Buddha Sons, An Explanation of (Śāntideva's) 'Engaging
in the Bodhisattva Deeds' by Gyel-tsap (rGyal-tshab)
Byang chub sems dpa'i spyod pa la 'jug pa'i rnam bshad rgyal sras
'jug ngogs
Essence of the Good Expositions, An Explanation of (Āryadeva's) 'Four
Hundred' by Gyel-tsap (rGyal-tshab)
bZhi brgya pa'i rnam bshad legs bshad snying po
Ocean of Reasoning, An Extensive Explanation of the Great Treatise
(Dharmakīrti's) 'Commentary on (Dignāga's) "Compendium on Valid
Cognisers"' by Kay-drup (mKhas-grub)
rGyas pa'i bstan bcos tshad ma rnam 'grel gyi rgya cher bshad pa rigs
pa'i rgya mtsho

Glossary

Abhidharma: Knowledge, the study of phenomena
Adhiprajñā: Higher wisdom
Adhisamādhi: Higher meditative stabilisation
Adhiśīla: Higher ethics
Anuttara-yoga: Highest Yoga, the fourth of the four sets of tantras
Arhan: Foe Destroyer
Ārya: Superior
Āryan: Superior, a person who has become elevated over common beings
    through directly cognising emptiness
Āyatana: Sources
Caryā: Performance, the second of the four sets of tantras
Dharma: That which holds, phenomenon, religious practice
Dharma-kāya: Truth Body, Body of Wisdom and of Nirvāna
Dhātu: Types
Hīnayāna: Lesser Vehicle
Kriyā: Action, the first of the four sets of tantras
Mahāyāna: Great Vehicle
Nirmāṇakāya: Emanation Body
Prajñā: Wisdom
Pratyekabuddha: Solitary Realiser
Rūpa-kāya: Form Body
Samādhi: Meditative stabilisation
Śamatha: Calm abiding
Śīla: Ethics
Skandha: Mental and physical aggregates
Śrāvaka: Hearer
Sūtrānta: Class of scripture
Tīrthika: Forder, a non-Buddhist propounding a ford or passage to
    liberation.
Triśikṣā: Three trainings
Vinaya: Discipline
Vipaśyanā: Special insight

Index

III

The Precious Garland
of Advice
for the King

(Sanskrit: Rājaparikathā-ratnamālā)

NĀGĀRJUNA

*Obeisance of the translators from Sanskrit
into Tibetan
Homage to all Buddhas and Bodhisattvas
Translated by Jeffrey Hopkins
and Lati Rimpoche*

Acknowledgements

The translators wish to thank Mr Gerald Yorke for many suggestions which improved the rendering in English.

Introduction

Nāgārjuna was an Indian pandit from Vidarbha in south India who lived approximately four hundred years after Buddha's death. At that time the Mahāyāna teaching had diminished, and Nāgārjuna assumed the task of reviving it by founding the Mādhyamika school of tenets. Here, in his *Precious Garland*, he clarifies the Buddha's exposition of emptiness based on the *Perfection of Wisdom Sūtras (Prajñāpāramitā)*. He presents the ten Bodhisattva stages leading to Buddhahood based on the *Sūtra on the Ten Stages (Daśabhūmika)*. He details a Bodhisattva's collections of merit and wisdom based on the *Sūtra Set Forth by Akṣayamati (Akṣayamatinirdeśa)*. The *Precious Garland* was intended primarily for the Indian king Śātavāhana, therefore, Nāgārjuna includes specific advice on ruling a kingdom. (The section on the undesirability of the body is written with reference to the female body simply because the king was a male. As Nāgārjuna says, the advice should be taken as applying to both males and females.) Among his works, the *Precious Garland* is renowned for extensively describing both the profound emptinesses and the extensive Bodhisattva deeds of compassion.

The translation is based on an oral transmission and explanation of the text received from His Holiness Tenzin Gyatso, the Fourteenth Dalai Lama, in Dharamsala, India in May of 1972. The text was translated in accordance with the commentary by Tsong-ka-pa's disciple Gyel-tsap (rGyal-tshab), whose guide has been included here to facilitate reading. The work was translated by Jeffrey Hopkins, who orally re-translated the English into Tibetan for verification and correction by Lati Rimpoche and then worked with Anne Klein to improve the presentation in English.

Chapter One

High Status and Definite Goodness

1 I bow down to the all-knowing,
   Freed from all defects,
   Adorned with all virtues,
   The sole friend of all beings.

2 O King, I will explain practices solely
   Virtuous to generate in you the doctrine,
   For the practices will be established
   In a vessel of the excellent doctrine.

3 In one who first practises high status
   Definite goodness arises later,
   For having attained high status one comes
   Gradually to definite goodness.

4 High status is thought of as happiness,
   Definite goodness as liberation,
   The quintessence of their means
   Are briefly faith and wisdom.

5 Through faith one relies on the practices,
   Through wisdom one truly knows,
   Of these two wisdom is the chief,
   Faith is its prerequisite.

6　He who does not neglect the practices
　　Through desire, hatred, fear or ignorance
　　Is known as one of faith, a superior
　　Vessel for definite goodness.

7　Having thoroughly analysed
　　All deeds of body, speech and mind,
　　He who realises what benefits self
　　And others and who always practises is wise.

8　Not killing, no longer stealing,
　　Forsaking the wives of others,
　　Refraining completely from false,
　　Divisive, harsh and senseless speech,

9　Forsaking covetousness, harmful
　　Intent and the views of Nihilists—
　　These are the ten white paths of
　　Action, their opposites are black.

10　Not drinking intoxicants, a good livelihood,
　　Non-harming, considerate giving, honouring
　　The honourable, and love—
　　Practice in brief is that.

11　Practice does not mean to
　　Mortify the body,
　　For one has not ceased to injure
　　Others and is not helping them.

12　He who does not esteem the great path of excellent
　　Doctrine which is bright with ethics, giving and patience,
　　Afflicts his body, takes
　　Bad paths like jungle trails;

13 His body entangled with vicious
   Afflictions, he enters for a long time
   The dreadful jungle of cyclic existence
   Among the trees of endless beings.

14 A short life comes through killing,
   Much suffering through harming,
   Through stealing poor resources,
   Through adultery enemies.

15 From lying arises slander,
   A parting of friends from divisiveness,
   From harshness hearing the unpleasant,
   From senselessness one's speech is not respected.

16 Covetousness destroys one's wishes,
   Harmful intent yields fright,
   Wrong views lead to bad views
   And drink to confusion of the mind.

17 Through not giving comes poverty,
   Through wrong livelihood, deception,
   Through arrogance a bad lineage,
   Through jealousy little beauty.

18 A bad colour comes through anger,
   Stupidity from not questioning
   The wise. The main fruit[1] of all this
   Is a bad migration for humans.

19 Opposite to the well known
   Fruits of these non-virtues
   Is a the arising of effects
   Caused by all the virtues.

20 Desire, hatred, ignorance and
   The actions they generate are non-virtues.
   Non-desire, non-hatred, non-ignorance
   And the actions they generate are virtues.

21 From non-virtues come all sufferings
   And likewise all bad migrations,
   From virtues all happy migrations
   And the pleasures of all births.

22 Desisting from all non-virtues
   And always engaging in virtues
   With body, speech and mind—these are
   Known as the three forms of practice.

23 Through these practices one is freed from becoming
   A hell-denizen, hungry ghost or animal;
   Reborn as a human or god one realises
   Extensive happiness, fortune and dominion.

24 Through the concentrations, immeasurables and form-
      lessnesses
   One experiences the bliss of Brahmā and so forth.
   Thus in brief are the practices
   For high status and their fruits.

25 The doctrines of definite goodness are
   Said by the Conquerors to be deep,
   Subtle and frightening to
   Children who are not learned.

26 'I am not, I will not be.
   I have not, I will not have',
   That frightens all children
   And kills fear in the wise.

27 By him who speaks only to help
Beings, it was said that they all
Have arisen from the conception of 'I'
And are enveloped with the conception of 'mine'.

28 'The "I" exists, the "mine" exists.'
These are wrong as ultimates,
For the two are not [established]
By a true and correct consciousness.

29 The mental and physical aggregates arise
From the conception of 'I' which is false in fact.[2]
How could what is grown
From a false seed be true?

30 Having thus seen the aggregates as untrue,
The conception of 'I' is abandoned
And due to this abandonment
The aggregates arise no more.

31 Just as it is said
That an image of one's face is seen
Depending on a mirror
But does not in fact exist [as a face],

32 So the conception of 'I' exists
Dependent on the aggregates,
But like the image of one's face
In reality the 'I' does not exist.

33 Just as without depending on a mirror
The image of one's face is not seen,
So too the 'I' does not exist
Without depending on the aggregates.

34 When the superior Ānanda had
   Attained [insight into] what this means,
   He won the eye of doctrine and taught it
   Continually to the monks.[3]

35 There is misconception of an 'I' as long
   As the aggregates are misconceived,
   When this conception of an 'I' exists,
   There is action which results in birth.

36 With these three pathways mutually causing each
   Other without a beginning, middle or an end,
   This wheel of cyclic existence
   Turns like the 'wheel' of a firebrand.

37 Because this wheel is not obtained from self, other
   Or from both, in the past, the present or the future,
   The conception of an 'I' ceases
   And thereby action and rebirth.

38 Thus one who sees how cause and effect
   Are produced and destroyed
   Does not regard the world
   As really existent or non-existent.

39 Thus one who has heard but does not examine
   The doctrine which destroys all suffering,
   And fears the fearless state
   Trembles due to ignorance.

40 That all these will not exist in nirvāṇa
   Does not frighten you [a Hīnayānist],
   Why does their non-existence
   Explained here cause you fright?

41 'In liberation there is no self and are no aggregates.'
   If liberation is asserted thus,
   Why is the removal here of the self
   And of the aggregates not liked by you?

42 If nirvāṇa is not a non-thing,
   Just how could it have thingness?
   The extinction of the misconception
   Of things and non-things is called nirvāṇa.

43 In brief the view of nihilism is
   That actions bear no fruits; without
   Merit and leading to a bad state,
   It is regarded as the wrong view.

44 In brief the view of existence
   Is that there are fruits of actions;
   Meritorious and conducive to happy
   Migrations, it is regarded as the right view.

45 Because 'is' and 'is not' are destroyed by wisdom,
   There is a passage beyond merit and sin,
   This, say the excellent, is liberation
   From both bad and happy migrations.

46 Seeing production[4] as caused
   One passes beyond non-existence,
   Seeing cessation as caused
   One no longer asserts existence.

47 Previously produced and simultaneously produced[5]
   [Causes] are non-causes; thus there are no causes in fact,
   Because [inherently existent] production is not
   Conventionally or ultimately known at all.

48 When this is, that arises,
    Like short when there is tall.
    When this is produced, so is that,
    Like light from a flame.

49 When there is tall, there must be short,
    They exist not through their own nature,
    Just as without a flame
    Light too does not arise.[5a]

50 Having thus seen that effects arise
    From causes, one asserts what appears
    In the conventions of the world
    And does not accept nihilism.

51 He who refutes [inherently existent cause
    And effect] does not develop [the view of] existence,
    [Asserting] as true what does not arise from conventions;
    Thereby one not relying on duality is liberated.

52 A form seen from a distance
    Is seen clearly by those nearby.
    If a mirage were water, why
    Is water not seen by those nearby?

53 The way this world is seen
    As real by those afar
    Is not so seen by those nearby
    [For whom it is] signless like a mirage.

54 Just as a mirage is like water but is
    Not water and does not in fact exist [as water],
    So the aggregates are like a self but are
    Not selves and do not in fact exist [as selves].

55 Having thought a mirage to be
Water and then having gone there,
He would just be stupid to surmise
'That water does not exist.'

56 One who conceives of the mirage-like
World that it does or does not exist
Is consequently ignorant. When there is
Ignorance, one is not liberated.

57 A follower of non-existence suffers bad migrations,
But happy ones accrue to followers of existence;
One who knows what is correct and true does not rely
On dualism and so becomes liberated.

58 If through knowing what is correct and true
He does not assert existence and non-existence
And thereby [you think] he believes in non-existence,
Why should he not be a follower of existence?

59 If from refuting [inherent] existence
Non-existence then accrues to him,
Why from refuting non-existence
Would existence not accrue to him?

60 Those who rely on enlightenment
Have no nihilistic thesis,
Behaviour or thought, how can
They be seen as nihilists?

61 Ask the worldly ones, the Sāṃkhyas,
Owl-Followers[6] and Nirgranthas,
The proponents of a person and aggregates,
If they propound what passes beyond 'is' and 'is not'.

62 Thereby know that the ambrosia
    Of the Buddhas' teaching is called profound,
    An uncommon doctrine passing
    Far beyond existence and non-existence.

63 Ultimately how could the world exist with a nature
    Which has gone beyond the past, the present
    And the future, not going when destroyed,
    Not coming and not staying even for an instant?

64 Because in reality there is
    No coming, going or staying,
    What ultimate difference is there
    Then between the world and nirvāṇa?

65 If there is no staying, there can be
    No production and no cessation.
    Then how could production, staying and
    Cessation ultimately exist?[7]

66 How are things non-momentary
    If they are always changing?
    If they do not change, then how
    In fact can they be altered?

67 Do they become momentary through
    Partial or complete disintegration?
    Because an inequality[8] is not apprehended,
    This momentariness cannot be admitted.

68 When a thing ceases to exist through momentariness,
    How can anything be old?
    When a thing is non-momentary due to constancy
    How can anything be old?

69 Since a moment ends it must have
A beginning and a middle,
This triple nature of a moment means
That the world never abides for an instant.

70 Also the beginning, middle and end
Are to be analysed like a moment;
Therefore, beginning, middle and end
Are not [produced] from self or other.

71 Due to having many parts 'one' does not exist,
There is not anything which is without parts,
Further without 'one' 'many' does not exist
And without existence there is no non-existence.

72 If through destruction or an antidote
An existent ceases to exist,
How could there be destruction or
An antidote without an existent?

73 Ultimately the world cannot
Through nirvāṇa disappear.
Asked whether it had an end
The Conqueror was silent.

74 Because he did not teach this profound doctrine
To worldly beings who were not receptacles,
The all-knowing one is therefore known
As omniscient by the wise.

75 Thus the doctrine of definite goodness
Was taught by the perfect Buddhas,
The seers of reality, as profound,
Unapprehendable and baseless.[9]

76 Frightened by this baseless doctrine,
Delighting in a base, not passing
Beyond existence and non-existence,
Unintelligent beings ruin themselves.

77 Afraid of the fearless abode,
Ruined, they ruin others.
O King, act in such a way
That the ruined do not ruin you.

78 O King, lest you be ruined
I will explain through the scriptures
The mode of the supramundane,
The reality that relies not on dualism.

79 This profundity which liberates
And is beyond both sin and virtue
Has not been tasted by those who fear the baseless,
The others, the Forders[10] and even by ourselves.

80 A person is not earth, not water,
Not fire, not wind, not space,
Not consciousness and not all of them;
What person is there other than these?

81 Just as the person is not an ultimate
But a composite of six constituents,
So too each of them in turn is a
Composite and not an ultimate.

82 The aggregates are not the self, they are not in it,
It is not in them, without them it is not,
It is not mixed with the aggregates like fire and fuel,[11]
Therefore how can the self exist?

83   The three elements[12] are not earth, they are not in it,
It is not in them, without them it is not;
Since this applies to each,
They like the self are false.

84   By themselves earth, water, fire and wind
Do not inherently exist;
When any three are absent, there cannot be one,
When one is absent, so too are the three.

85   If when three are absent, the one does not exist
And if when one is absent, the three do not exist,
Then each itself does not exist;
How can they produce a composite?

86   Otherwise if each itself exists,
Why without fuel is there no fire?
Likewise why is there no water, wind or earth
Without motility, hardness or cohesion?

87   If [it is answered that] fire is well known [not to exist
Without fuel but the other three elements exist
Independently], how could your three exist in themselves
Without the others? It is impossible for the three
Not to accord with dependent-arising.

88   How can those existing by themselves
Be mutually dependent?
How can those which exist not by themselves
Be mutually dependent?

89   If as individuals they do not exist,
But where there is one, the other three are there,
Then if unmixed, they are not in one place,
And if mixed, they cease to be individuals.

90 The elements do not themselves exist individually,
So how could their own individual characters do so?
What do not themselves individually exist cannot pre-
   dominate;[13]
Their characters are regarded as conventionalities.

91 This mode of refutation is also to be applied
To colours, odours, tastes and objects of touch,
Eye, consciousness and form,
Ignorance, action and birth,

92 Agent, object, acting and number,
Possession, cause, effect and time,
Short and long and so forth,
Name and name-bearer as well.

93 Earth, water, fire and wind,
Tall and short, subtle and coarse
Virtue and so forth are said by the Subduer
To cease in the consciousness [of reality].

94 The spheres of earth, water, fire
And wind do not appear to that
Undemonstrable consciousness,
Complete lord over the limitless.

95 Here tall and short, subtle and coarse,
Virtue and non-virtue
And here names and forms
All cease to be.

96 What was not known is known
To consciousness as [the reality of] all
That appeared before. Thereby these phenomena
Later cease to be in consciousness.

97   All these phenomena related to beings
     Are seen as fuel for the fire of consciousness,
     They are consumed through being burned
     By the light of true discrimination.

98   The reality is later ascertained
     Of what was formerly imputed by ignorance;
     When a thing is not found,
     How can there be a non-thing?

99   Because the phenomena of forms are
     Only names, space too is only a name;
     Without the elements how could forms exist?
     Therefore even 'name-only' does not exist.

100 Feelings, discriminations, factors of composition
     And consciousnesses are to be considered
     Like the elements and the self, thereby
     The six constituents[14] are selfless.

Chapter Two

An Interwoven Explanation of Definite Goodness and High Status

101 Just as there is nothing when
     A banana tree with all its parts
     Is torn apart, it is the same when a person
     Is divided into the [six] constituents.[15]

102 Therefore the Conquerors said,
     'All phenomena are selfless.'
     Since this is so, you must accept
     All six constituents as selfless.

103 Thus neither self nor non-self
     Are understood as real,
     Therefore the Great Subduer rejected
     The views of self and non-self.

104 Sights, sounds and so forth were said by the Subduer
     Neither to be true nor false;
     If from one position its opposite arises,
     Both in fact do not exist.[16]

105 Thus ultimately this world
     Is beyond truth and falsehood,
     Therefore he does not assert
     That it really is or is not.

106   [Knowing that] these in all ways do not exist,
How could the All-Knower say
They have limits or no limits,
Or have both or neither?

107   'Innumerable Buddhas have come, will come and are
Here at present; there are tens of millions of sentient
Beings, but the Buddhas will abide
In the past, the present and the future;

108   'The extinguishing of the world in the three
Times does not cause it to increase,[17]
Then why was the All-Knower silent
About the limits of the world?'

109   That which is secret for a common
Being is the profound doctrine,
The illusory nature of the world,
The ambrosia of the Buddha's teaching.

110   Just as the production and disintegration
Of an illusory elephant are seen,
But the production and disintegration
Do not really exist,

111   So the production and disintegration
Of the illusory world are seen,
But the production and disintegration
Ultimately do not exist.

112   Just as an illusory elephant,
But a bewildering of consciousness,
Comes not from anywhere,
Goes not, nor really stays,

113 So this world of illusion,
A bewildering of consciousness,
Comes not from anywhere,
Goes not, nor really stays.

114 Thus it has a nature beyond time;
Other than as a convention
What world is there in fact
Which would be 'is' or 'is not'?

115 This was why the Buddha
At all times kept silent
About the fourfold format: with or
Without a limit, both or neither.[18]

116 When the body, which is unclean,
Coarse, an object of the senses,
Does not stay in the mind [as unclean],
Although it is all the time in view,

117 Then how could this doctrine
Which is most subtle, profound,
Baseless and not manifest,
Appear with ease to the mind?

118 Realising that this doctrine is too
Profound and hard to understand,
The Buddha, the Subduer,
Turned away from teaching it.

119 This doctrine wrongly understood
Ruins the unwise,[19] because
They sink into the filth
Of nihilistic views.

120 Further, the stupid who fancy
Themselves wise,[20] having a nature
Ruined by rejecting [emptiness] fall headfirst
To a fearful hell from their wrong understanding.

121 Just as one comes to ruin
Through wrong eating and obtains
Long life, freedom from disease,
Strength and pleasure through right eating,

122 So one comes to ruin
Through wrong understanding
But gains bliss and complete enlightenment
Through right understanding.

123 Therefore having forsaken all nihilistic
Views and rejections concerning emptiness,
Strive your best to understand correctly
For the sake of achieving all your aims.

124 If this doctrine is not truly understood,
The conception of an 'I' prevails,
Hence come virtuous and non-virtuous actions
Which give rise to good and bad rebirths.

125 So long then as the doctrine that destroys
The misconception of an 'I' is not known,
Take care always to practise
Giving, ethics and patience.

126 A king who performs actions
With their prior, intermediary
And final practices
Is not harmed here or in the future.

127 Here through the practices come fame and happiness,
There is no fear now or at the point of death,
In the next life flourishes happiness,
Therefore always observe the practices.

128 The practices are the best policy,
It is through them that the world is pleased;
Neither here nor in the future is one
Cheated by a world that has been pleased.

129 The world is displeased
By the policies of non-practice;
Due to the displeasure of the world
One is not pleased here or in the future.

130 How could those of bad understanding
On a path to bad migrations, wretched,
Intent on deceiving others, having
Wrong aims, understand what is meaningful?

131 How could one intent on deceiving
Others be a man of policy?
Through it he will be cheated
In many thousands of births.

132 One who seeks disfavour for an enemy
Should neglect his faults and observe his virtues,
That brings help to oneself
And disfavour to the foe.

133 You should cause the religious
And the worldly to assemble
Through giving, speaking pleasantly,
Behaving with purpose and concordance.[21]

134   Just as by themselves the true words
     Of kings generate firm trust,
     So their false words are the best means
     To create distrust.

135   What is not deceitful is the truth
     And not a fabrication of the mind,
     What to others is solely helpful is the truth,
     The opposite is falsehood since it does not help.

136   Just as one splendid charity
     Conceals the faults of kings,
     So avarice destroys
     All their wealth.

137   In peace there is profundity
     From which the highest respect arises,
     From respect come power and command,
     Therefore observe peace.

138   From wisdom comes a mind unshakeable,
     Relying not on others, firm
     And not deceived, therefore,
     O King, be intent on wisdom.

139   A lord of men having the four goodnesses,
     Truth, giving, peace and wisdom,
     Is praised by gods and men
     As are the four good practices themselves.

140   Wisdom and practice always grow
     For one who keeps company
     With those whose speech is beneficial, who are pure,
     Wise, compassionate and not contaminated.

141 Rare are helpful speakers,
     Listeners are rarer,
     But rarer still are words
     Which though unpleasant help at once.

142 Therefore having realised the unpleasant
     As being helpful, act on it quickly,
     Just as when ill one takes nauseous
     Medicine from one of a loving nature.

143 Always considering that life, health
     And dominion are impermanent,
     You will make an intense effort
     Just to carry out the practices.

144 Seeing that death is certain, that
     When dead one suffers from one's sins,
     You should not sin, although
     There might be passing pleasure.

145 Sometimes horror is seen
     And sometimes it is not,[22]
     If there is comfort in one,
     Why fear you not the other?

146 Intoxicants lead to worldly scorn,
     Affairs are ruined, wealth is wasted,
     The unsuitable is done from delusion,
     Therefore never take intoxicants.

147 Gambling causes avarice,
     Unpleasantness, hatred, deception, cheating,
     Wildness, lying, senseless and harsh speech,
     Therefore never gamble.

148 Lust for a woman mostly comes
From thinking that her body is clean,
But there is nothing clean
In a woman's body.

149 The mouth is a vessel filled with foul
Saliva and filth between the teeth,
The nose with fluids, snot and mucus,
The eyes with their own filth and tears.

150 The body is a vessel filled
With excrement, urine, lungs and liver;
He whose vision is obscured and does not see
A woman thus, lusts for her body.

151 Just as some fools desire
An ornamented pot of filth,
So the ignorant and obscured
And the worldly desire women.

152 If the world is greatly attached
To the nauseous stinking body
Which should cause loss of attachment,
How can it be led to freedom from desire?

153 Just as pigs yearn greatly for
A source of excrement, urine and vomit,
So some lustful ones desire
A source of excrement, urine and vomit.

154 This filthy city of a body,
With protruding holes for the elements
Is called by stupid beings
An object of pleasure.

155   Once you have seen for yourself the filth
      Of excrement, urine and so forth,
      How could you be attracted
      To a body so composed?

156   Why should you lust desirously for this
      While recognising it as a filthy form
      Produced by a seed whose essence is filth,
      A mixture of blood and semen?

157   He who lies on the filthy mass
      Covered by skin moistened with
      Those fluids, merely lies
      On top of a woman's bladder.

158   If whether beautiful or
      Ugly, whether old or young,
      All the bodies of women are filthy
      From what attributes does your lust arise?

159   Just as it is not fit to desire
      Filth although it have a good colour
      And shape in its very freshness,
      So is it with a woman's body.

160   How could the nature of this putrid corpse,
      A rotten mass covered outside by skin,
      Not be seen when it looks
      So very horrible?

161   'The skin is not foul,
      It is like a cloak.'
      Over a mass of filth
      How could it be clean?

162 A pot though beautiful outside
      Is reviled when filled with filth.
      Why is the body, when so filled
      And foul by nature, not reviled?

163 If against filth you revile,
      Why not against this body
      Which befouls clean scents,
      Garlands, food and drink?

164 Just as one's own or others'
      Filthiness is reviled,
      Why not revile against one's own
      And others' filthy bodies?

165 Since your own body is
      As filthy as a woman's,
      Should not you abandon
      Desire for self and other?

166 If you yourself wash this body
      Dripping from the nine wounds[23]
      And still do not think it filthy, what
      Use have you for profound instruction?

167 Whoever composes poetry with
      Metaphors which elevate this body—
      O how shameless! O how stupid!
      How embarrassing before the wise!

168 Since these sentient beings are obscured
      By the darkness of ignorance,
      They quarrel mostly over what they want
      Like dogs for the sake of some filth.

169   There is pleasure when a sore is scratched,
       But to be without sores is more pleasurable still;
       There are pleasures in worldly desires,
       But to be without desires is more pleasurable still.

170   If you thus analyse, even though
       You do not become free from desire,
       Because your desire has lessened
       You will no longer lust for women.

171   To hunt game is an endless
       Cause of a short life,
       Suffering and hell,
       Therefore always keep from killing.

172   Bad like a snake with poisonous
       Fangs, its body stained with filth,
       Is he who frightens embodied
       Beings when he encounters them.

173   Just as farmers are gladdened
       When a great rain-cloud gathers,
       So one who gladdens embodied beings
       When he encounters them is good.

174   Thus always observe the practices
       And not those counter to them.

         *   *   *   *   *   *

       If you and the world wish to gain
       The highest enlightenment,

175   Its roots are the altruistic aspiration
       To enlightenment firm like Meru, the king of mountains,
       The compassion which reaches to all quarters,
       The wisdom which relies not on duality.

176 O great King, listen to how
Your body will be adorned
With the two and thirty
Signs of a great being.

177 Through the proper honouring of reliquaries,[24]
Honourable beings, superiors and the elderly
You will become a Universal Monarch,
Your glorious hands and feet marked with [a design of]
wheels.

178 O King, always maintain firmly
What you have vowed about the practices,
You will then become a Bodhisattva
With feet that are very level.

179 Through gifts and pleasant speech,
Purposeful and concordant behaviour
You will have hands with glorious
Fingers joined by webs [of light].

180 Through abundant giving
Of the best food and drink
Your glorious hands and feet will be soft;
Your hands and feet and shoulder blades
And the nape of your neck will broaden,
So your body will be big and those seven areas broad.

181 Through never doing harm and freeing the condemned
Beautiful will be your body, straight and large,
Very tall with long fingers
And broad backs of the heels.

182 Through promoting the vowed practices
Your good colour will be glorious,
Your ankles will not be prominent,
Your body hairs will grow upwards.

183 Through your zeal for knowledge and the arts
And so forth, and through imparting them
You will have the calves of an antelope,
A sharp mind and great wisdom.

184 If others seek your wealth and possessions,
Through the discipline of immediate giving
You will have broad hands, a pleasant complexion
And will become a leader of the world.

185 Through reconciling well
Friends who have been divided
Your glorious secret organ
Will retract inside.

186 Through giving good houses
And nice comfortable carpets
Your colour will be very soft
Like pure stainless gold.

187 Through giving the highest powers [or kingdoms]
And following a teacher properly
You will be adorned by each and every hair
And by a circle of hair between the eyebrows.

188 Through speech that is pleasant and pleasing
And by acting upon the good speech [of others]
You will have curving shoulders
And a lion-like upper body.

189 If you nurse and cure the sick,
Your chest will be broad,
You will live naturally
And all tastes will be the best.

190 Through initiating activities concordant
With the practices, the swelling on your crown[24a]
Will stand out well and [your body] will be
Symmetrical like a banyan tree.

191 Through speaking true and soft words
Over the years, O lord of men,
Your tongue will be long and
Your voice that of Brahmā.

192 Through speaking true words
Always at all times
You will have cheeks like a lion,
Be glorious and hard to best.

193 Through showing great respect, serving
Others and doing what should be done,
Your teeth will shine
Very white and even.

194 Through using true and non-divisive
Speech over a long time
You will have forty glorious teeth
Set evenly and good.

195 Through viewing things with love
And without desire, hatred or delusion
Your eyes will be bright and blue
With eyelashes like a bull.

196 Thus in brief know well
These two and thirty signs
Of a great lion of a being
Together with their causes.

197 The eighty minor marks arise
From a concordant cause of love;
Fearing this text would be too long,
I will not, O King, explain them.

198 All Universal Emperors
Are regarded as having these,
But their purity, their lustre and beauty
Cannot begin to match those of a Buddha.

199 The good major and minor marks
Of a Universal Emperor
Are said to arise from a single act
Of faith in the King of Subduers.

200 But such virtue accumulated with a mind
One-pointed for a hundred times ten million aeons
Cannot produce even one
Of the hair-pores of a Buddha.
Just as the brilliance of suns
Is slightly like that of fireflies,
So the signs of a Buddha are slightly like
Those of a Universal Emperor.

Chapter Three
The Collections for Enlightenment

201 Great King, hear how from the great
Scriptures of the Mahāyāna
The marks of a Buddha arise
From merit inconceivable.

202 The merit which creates all Solitary
Realisers, Learners and Non-Learners
And all the merit of the transient world
Is measureless like the universe itself.

203 Through such merit ten times extended
One hair-pore of a Buddha is achieved;
All the hair-pores of a Buddha
Arise in just the same way.

204 Through multiplying by a hundred
The merit which produces
All the hair-pores of a Buddha
One auspicious minor mark is won.

205 O King, as much merit as is required
For one auspicious minor mark,
So much also is required
For each up to the eightieth.

206   Through multiplying by a hundred
       The collection of merit which achieves
       The eighty auspicious minor marks
       One major sign of a great being arises.

207   Through multiplying by a thousand
       The extensive merit which is the cause
       Of achieving the thirty minor signs
       The hair-treasure like a full moon arises.[25]

208   Through multiplying by a hundred thousand
       The merit for the hair-treasure
       A protector's crown-protrusion
       Is produced, imperceptible [as to size].

       [Through increasing by ten million times a hundred
       Thousand the merit for the crown-protrusion
       There comes the excellence which gives the euphony
       Of a Buddha's speech and its sixty qualities.][26]

209   Though such merit is measureless
       For brevity it is said to have a measure
       And all of it is said to be
       Ten times the merit of the world.

210   When the causes of even the Form Body
       Of a Buddha are immeasurable
       As the world, how then could the causes
       Of the Body of Truth be measured?

211   If the causes of all things are small
       But they produce extensive effects,
       The thought that the measureless causes of Buddhahood
       Have measurable effects must be eliminated.

212 The Form Body of a Buddha
Arises from collected merit,
The Body of Truth in brief, O King,
Arises from collected wisdom.

213 Thus these two collections cause
Buddhahood to be attained,
So in brief always rely
Upon merit and wisdom.

214 Do not be lazy about this [amassing]
Of merit to achieve enlightenment
Since reasoning and scripture
Can restore one's spirits.

215 Just as in all directions
Space, earth, water, fire and wind
Are without limit, so suffering
Sentient beings are limitless.

216 The Bodhisattvas through their compassion
Lead these limitless sentient beings
Out of suffering and establish
Them definitely in Buddhahood.

217 Whether sleeping or not sleeping,
After thoroughly assuming [such compassion]
He who remains steadfast,
Even though he might become non-conscientious,

218 Always accumulates merit as limitless as all
Sentient beings, for their number has no limit.
Know then that since [the causes] are limitless
Limitless Buddhahood is not hard to attain.

219 [A Bodhisattva] stays for a limitless time [in the world],
For limitless embodied beings he seeks
The limitless [qualities of] enlightenment
And performs virtuous actions without limit.

220 Though enlightenment is limitless,
How could he not attain it
With these four limitless collections
Without being delayed for long?

221 The limitless collections
Of merit and wisdom
Eradicate most quickly
The sufferings of mind and body.

222 The physical sufferings of bad migrations
Such as hunger and thirst arise from sins;
A Bodhisattva does not sin and through his merit
Does not [suffer physically] in other lives.

223 The mental sufferings of desire,
Fear, avarice and so forth arise
From obscuration; he knows them to be baseless
And so can uproot quickly [all mental suffering].

224 Since he is not greatly harmed
By physical and mental pain,
Why should he be discouraged even though
He leads the worldly beings in all worlds?

225 It is hard to bear suffering even for a little,
What need is there to speak of doing so for long?
What can ever harm a happy man
Who never suffers for an instant?

226 If his body does not suffer,
How can he suffer in his mind?
Through his great compassion he feels pain
For the world and so stays in it long.[27]

227 Do not then be lazy thinking
Buddhahood is far away.
Always strive hard for these collections
To wipe out faults and attain virtues.

228 Realising that ignorance, desire
And hatred are defects, forsake them completely.
Realise that non-desire, non-hatred and non-ignorance
Are virtues and so practise them with vigour.

229 Through desire one is reborn a hungry ghost,
Through hatred in a hell, through ignorance
Mostly as an animal; through stopping these
One becomes a god or a human being.

230 To eliminate all defects and maintain
The virtues are the practices of high status;
To wipe out all misconceptions through the conscious-
ness
[Of reality] is the practice of definite goodness.

231 With respect and without stint you should construct
Images of Buddha, reliquaries and temples
And provide abundant riches,
Food, necessities and so forth.

232 Please construct from all precious substances
Images of Buddha with fine proportions,
Well designed and sitting on lotuses
Adorned with all precious substances.

233   You should sustain with all endeavour
      The excellent doctrine and the assembly
      Of monks, and decorate reliquaries
      With gold and jewelled friezes.

234   Revere the reliquaries
      With gold and silver flowers,
      Diamonds, corals, pearls,
      Emeralds, cat's eye gems and sapphires.

235   To revere the teachers of the doctrine
      Is to do what pleases them,
      [Offering] goods and services
      And relying firmly on the doctrine.[28]

236   Listen to a teacher with homage
      And respect, serve and pray to him.
      Always respectfully revere
      The [other] Bodhisattvas.

237   You should not respect, revere
      Or do homage to others, the Forders,[29]
      Because through that the ignorant
      Would become enamoured of the faulty.

238   You should make donations of the word
      Of the King of Subduers and of the treatises
      He gave, as well as pages and books along
      With their prerequisites, the pens and ink.

239   As a way to increase wisdom
      Wherever there is a school
      Provide for the livelihood of teachers
      And bestow estates [for their provision].

240　In order to root out the suffering
　　Of sentient beings, the old, young and infirm,
　　You should establish through your influence
　　Barbers and doctors in your kingdom.

241　Please act with good wisdom and provide
　　Hostels, amusement centres, dikes,
　　Ponds, rest-houses, water-vessels,
　　Beds, food, grass and wood.

242　Please establish rest-houses
　　In all temples, towns and cities
　　And provide water-vessels
　　On all arid roadways.

243　Always care compassionately for
　　The sick, the unprotected, those stricken
　　With suffering, the lowly and the poor
　　And take special care to nourish them.

244　Until you have given to monks and beggars
　　Seasonally appropriate food
　　And drink, produce, grain and fruit,
　　You should not partake of them.

245　At the sites of the water-vessels
　　Place shoes, umbrellas, water-filters,
　　Tweezers for removing
　　Thorns, needles, thread and fans.

246　Within the vessels place the three medicinal
　　Fruits, the three fever medicines, butter,
　　Honey, salve for the eyes and antidotes
　　To poison, written spells and prescriptions.[30]

247   At the sites of the vessels place
      Salves for the body, feet and head,
      Wool, small chairs, gruel, jars,
      Pots, axes and so forth.

248   Please have small containers
      In the shade filled with sesame,
      Rice, grains, foods, molasses
      And suitable water.

249   At the openings of ant-hills
      Please have trustworthy men
      Always put food and water,
      Sugar and piles of grain.

250   Before and after taking food
      Offer appropriate fare
      To hungry ghosts, dogs,
      Ants, birds and so forth.

251   Provide extensive care
      For the persecuted, the victims [of disasters],
      The stricken and diseased,
      And for the worldly beings in conquered areas.

252   Provide stricken farmers
      With seeds and sustenance,
      Eliminate high taxes
      By reducing their rate.

253   Protect [the poor] from the pain of wanting [your
        wealth],
      Set up no [new] tolls and reduce those [that are heavy],
      Free them from the suffering [that follows when
      The tax collector] is waiting at the door.

254 Eliminate thieves and robbers
In your own and others' countries.
Please set prices fairly and keep
Profits level [when things are scarce].

255 You should know full well [the counsel]
That your ministers have offered,
And should always follow it
If it benefits the world.

256 Just as you love to think
What could be done to help yourself,
So should you love to think
What could be done to help others.

257 If only for a moment make yourself
Available for the use of others
Just as earth, water, fire, wind, medicine
And forests [are available to all].

258 Even during the time needed to take seven steps
Merit measureless as the sky
Is produced in Bodhisattvas
Who are well disposed to giving wealth away.

259 If you give to the needy
Girls of beauty well adorned,
You will thereby master the spells
To retain the excellent doctrine.

260 Formerly the Subduer provided
Along with every need and so forth
Eighty thousand girls
With all adornments.

261 Lovingly give to beggars
     Various and glittering
     Clothes, ornaments, perfumes,
     Garlands and enjoyments.

262 If you provide [facilities]
     For those most deprived who lack
     The means [to study] the doctrine,
     There is no greater gift than that.

263 Even give poison to
     Those whom it will help,
     But do not give the best food
     To those whom it will not help.

264 Just as some say that it will help
     A cut finger to hold a snake,
     So it is said that the Subduer
     Brings discomfort to help others.

265 You should respect most highly
     The excellent doctrine and its teachers,
     You should listen reverently to it
     And then give it to others.

266 Take no pleasure in worldly talk, but take
     Delight in what passes beyond the world,
     Cause good qualities to generate in others
     In the same way that you wish them for yourself.

267 Please be not satisfied with the doctrines you have
     Heard, but retain the meanings and discriminate.
     Please always make great effort
     To offer teachers presents.

268 Recite not from the worldly Nihilists,
Stop debating in the interests of pride,
Praise not your own good qualities,
But stress those even of your foes.

269 Do not say what hurts,
With evil intent talk
Not of others, analyse
Your own mistakes yourself.

270 You should free yourself completely from
The faults the wise decry in others,
And through your power cause
Others to do the same.

271 Consider the harm done to you by others
As created by your former deeds, be not angry,
Act in such a way that you do not cause
More suffering and your own faults will disappear.

272 Provide help to others
Without hope of reward,
Bear suffering alone and
Share your pleasures with beggars.

273 Do not be inflated even when you have acquired
The prosperity of gods.
Do not even be depressed
By the disadvantageous poverty of hungry ghosts.

274 For your own sake always speak the truth.
Even should it cause your death
Or ruin your kingdom,
Do not speak in any other way.

275   Always observe the discipline
Of actions as it has been explained,
Then, O glorious one, you will become
The best of models upon earth.

276   You should always well analyse
Everything before you act,
Through seeing things just as they are
You will not rely on others.

277   Through these practices your kingdom will be happy,
A broad canopy of fame
Will rise in all directions,
And your ministers will revere you completely.

278   The causes of death are many,
Those of staying alive are few,
These too can become the causes of death,
Therefore always perform the practices.

279   If you carry out the practices,
The mental happiness which arises
In the world and yourself
Is most beneficial.

280   Through the practices you will
Sleep and awaken in happiness;
Faultless in your inner nature
Happy will even be your dreams.

281   Intent on serving your parents, respectful
To the principals of your lineage,
Using your resources well, patient, generous,
With kindly speech, without divisiveness and truthful,

282 Through performing such discipline for one
Lifetime you will become a king of gods;
As such you will do still more,
Therefore observe such practices.

283 Even three times a day to offer
Three hundred cooking pots of food
Does not match a portion of the merit
Acquired in one instant of love.

284 Though [through love] you are not liberated
You will attain the eight virtues of love,
Gods and humans will be friendly,
Even [non-humans] will protect you,

285 You will have pleasures of the mind and many
[Of the body], poison and weapons will not harm you,
Effortlessly will you attain your aims
And be reborn in the world of Brahmā.

286 If you cause sentient beings to generate
The aspiration to enlightenment and make it firm,
Your own aspiration will always be
To enlightenment firm like [Meru] king of mountains.

287 Through faith you will not be without leisure,
Through good ethics you will have good migrations,
Through becoming familiar with emptiness
You will be unattached to all phenomena.

288 Through not wavering you will attain awareness,
And intelligence through thinking; through respect
You will realise what the doctrines mean,
Through their retention you will become wise.

289   Through not causing the hearing and the giving
      Of the doctrine to be obscured
      You will company with Buddhas
      And will quickly attain your wish.

290   Through non-attachment you will learn what [the doctrines] mean,
      Through not being miserly your resources will increase,
      Through not being proud you will become chief [of those respected],
      Through enduring the doctrine you will attain retention.

291   Through giving the five essentials[31]
      As well as non-fright to the frightened
      No evil will there be to harm you,
      Of the mighty you will be the best.

292   Through offering many lamps
      At reliquaries and elsewhere
      And oil for lamps in dark places
      Your divine eye will open.

293   Through offering bells and instruments
      For the worship of reliquaries
      And elsewhere drums and trumpets,
      Your divine ear will open.

294   Through not relating others' mistakes
      And not talking of their defective limbs,
      But protecting their minds, you will gain
      Knowledge of the minds of others.

295   Through giving conveyances and shoes,
Through serving the feeble and through
Providing teachers with youths you will acquire
The skill to create magical emanations.[32]

296   Through acting to promote the doctrine,[33]
Remembering its books and their meaning,
And through stainless giving of the doctrine
You will remember your continuum of lives.

297   Through knowing thoroughly, correctly and truly
That no phenomena inherently exist,
You will attain the sixth clairvoyance
That extinguishes all contamination well.

298   Through cultivating the wisdom of reality which is
The same [for all phenomena] and is moistened with
    compassion
For the sake of liberating all sentient beings,
You will become a Conqueror with all the excellences.

299   Through various pure aspirations
Your Buddha Land will be purified,
Through offering gems to the King
Of Subduers you will give out infinite light.

300   Therefore knowing how actions
And their effects agree,
For your own sake help beings
Always and so help yourself.

Chapter Four

Royal Policy

301 A king who does what is not righteous
And not suitable is mostly praised
By his subjects, for it is hard to know
What he will or will not tolerate;
Therefore it is hard to know
What is useful or not [to say].[34]

302 If useful but unpleasant words
Are hard to speak to someone else,
What could I, a monk, say to a king
Who is a lord of the great earth?

303 But because of my affection for you
And through my compassion for all beings,
I tell you without hesitation
That which is useful but unpleasant.

304 The Blessed One said that students are to be told
The truth, gentle, meaningful and salutary,
At the proper time and from compassion.
That is why you are being told all this.

305 O steadfast one, if true words
Are spoken without anger,
One should take them as fit to be
Heard, like water fit for bathing.

306 Realise that I am telling you
What is useful here and later.
Act on it so as to help
Yourself and also others.

307 If you do not make contributions
Of the wealth obtained from former giving,
Through your ingratitude and attachment
You will not obtain wealth in the future.

308 Here in the world workers do not carry
Provisions for a journey unpaid.
In the same way lowly beggars who carry [what you
    give them] multiplied
A hundred times for your future life will not do so
    without payment.

309 Always be of exalted mind
Delighting in exalted deeds,
From exalted actions arise
All effects that are exalted.

310 Create centres of doctrine, abodes
Of the Three Jewels and fame
And glory which lowly kings
Have not even conceived in their minds.

311 O King, it is best not to create
Centres of doctrine which do not stir
The hairs of neighbouring kings because
Of ill repute even after death.

312 Use even all your wealth to cause
The exalted to become free
From pride, and [the equal] to become delighted and to
     overcome
The inclinations of the lowly through your great
     exaltation.[35]

313 Having let go of all possessions
[At death] powerless you must go elsewhere,
But all that has been used for the doctrine
Precedes you [as good karma].

314 All the possessions of a previous king
Come under the control of his successor
Of what use are they then to the former
King for practice, happiness or fame?

315 Through using wealth there is happiness here and now,
Through giving there is happiness in the future,
From wasting it without using it or giving it away,
There is only misery. How could there be happiness?

316 Because of lack of power while dying, you will be
Unable to give by way of your ministers,
Shamelessly they will lose affection
For you and will seek to please the new king.

317 Therefore while in good health create now
Centres of doctrine with all your wealth,
For you are living amidst the causes
Of death like a lamp standing in a breeze.

318 Also other centres of doctrine
Established by the previous king,
All the temples and so forth,
Should be sustained as before.

319 Please have them attended by those
Who harm not others, keep their vows,
Are virtuous, truthful, kind to visitors,
Patient, non-combative and always industrious.

320 Cause the blind, the sick, the lowly,
The protectorless, the wretched
And the crippled equally to attain
Food and drink without interruption.

321 Provide all types of support
For practitioners who do not seek it
And even for those living
In the realms of other kings.

322 At all centres of the doctrine
Appoint attendants who are
Energetic, without greed, skilful,
Religious and not harmful.

323 Appoint ministers who know good policy,
Who practise the doctrine, are affectionate,
Pure, friendly, undaunted, of good lineage,
Of excellent disposition and grateful.

324 Appoint generals who are generous,
Without attachments, brave, affectionate,
Who use [the king's wealth] properly, are steadfast,
Always attentive and practise the doctrine.

325 Appoint as administrators men who are old,
     Of religious disposition, pure and able,
     Who know what should be done, are well read, unbiased,
     Affectionate and understand good policy.

326 Every month you should hear from them
     About all the income and expenses
     And having heard you should tell then all that should
     Be done for the centres of doctrine and so forth.

327 If your kingdom exists for the doctrine
     And not for fame or desire,
     Then it will be extremely fruitful,
     If not its fruit will be misfortune.

328 O lord of men, since in this world
     Most are prone to deceive each other,
     Listen to how your kingdom
     And your practice should be.

329 Let there always be around you many men
     Old in experience, of good lineage,
     Who know what policy is good, shrink from sin,
     Are agreeable and know what should be done.

330 Even if they rightfully have fined,
     Bound or punished people and so forth,
     You, being softened with compassion,
     Should always take care [of the offenders].

331 O King, through compassion you should always
     Generate an attitude of help
     Even for all those embodied beings
     Who have committed appalling sins.

332 Especially generate compassion
For those murderers, whose sins are horrible;
Those of fallen nature are receptacles
Of compassion from those whose nature is great.

333 Free the weaker prisoners
After a day or five days,
Do not think the others
Are never to be freed.

334 For each one whom you do not think
To free you will lose the layman's vow,
Because you will have lost the vow
Faults will constantly be amassed.

335 As long as the prisoners are not freed,
They should be made comfortable
With barbers, baths, food, drink,
Medicine and clothing.[36]

336 Just as unworthy sons are punished
Out of a wish to make them worthy,
So punishment should be enforced with compassion
And not through hatred or desire for wealth.

337 Once you have analysed the angry
Murderers and recognised them well,
You should banish them without
Killing or tormenting them.

338 In order to maintain control, oversee your country
Through the eyes of agents;
Attentive and mindful
Always do those things that accord with the practices.

339 Continually honour in an exalted way
Those who are well grounded in good qualities
With gifts, respect and reverence,
And likewise honour all the rest.

340 The birds of the populace will alight upon
The royal tree which provides the shade of patience,
The flourishing flowers of respect
And large fruits of resplendent giving.

341 A king whose nature is to give
Is liked if he is strong,
Like a sugared pastry
Hardened with cardamom pepper.

342 If you analyse and reason thus
Your dominion will not degenerate,
It will not be without principle
Nor become a system without rule.

343 You did not bring your kingdom with you from your
Former life nor will you take it to the next,
Since it was won by virtues, to act
For it without virtue is wrong.

344 O King, exert yourself
To avert a succession
Of miserable supplies for the kingdom
Through [misuse of] the royal resources.

345 O King, exert yourself
To increase the succession
Of the kingdom's resources
Through [proper use of] your own.

346 Although a Universal Monarch rules
Over the four continents, his pleasures
Are regarded as only two,
The physical and the mental.

347 Physical feelings of pleasure
Are only a lessening of pain,
Mental pleasures are made by thought,
Created only by the intellect.

348 All the wealth of worldly pleasures
Are but a lessening of suffering,
Or are only [creations of] thought,
Thus they are in fact not real.

349 One by one there is enjoyment of
Continents, countries, towns and homes,
Conveyances, seats, clothing, beds, food,
Drink, elephants, horses and women.

350 When the mind has any [one of these
As its object] there is said to be
Pleasure, but if no attention is paid to the others,
The others are not then in fact real [causes of pleasure].

351 When [all] five senses, eye and so forth,
[Simultaneously] apprehend their objects,
A thought [of pleasure] does not refer [to all of them],
Therefore at that time they do not all give pleasure.

352 Whenever any of the [five] objects is known
[As pleasurable] by one of the [five] senses,
Then the remaining [objects] are not so known[37]
Since they are not real [causes of pleasure].

353   When the mind apprehends a past object
Which has been picked up by the senses,
It imagines and fancies
It to be pleasurable.

354   Also the one sense which here [in the world
Is said to] know one object,
Without an object is as unreal
As that object is without it.

355   Just as a child is said to be born
Dependent on a father and mother,
So a consciousness is said to arise
Dependent on a sense and on a form.

356   Past and future objects
And the senses are unreal,
So too are present [objects] since
They are not distinct from these two.[38]

357   Just as due to error the eye perceives
A [whirling] firebrand as a wheel,
So the senses apprehend
Present objects [as if real].

358   The senses and their objects are regarded
As being composed of the elements,
Since the individual elements
Are unreal, so too are those objects.

359   If each element is different
It follows that there could be fire without fuel,
If mixed they would be characterless[39]
And this is true of the other elements.

360 Because the elements are unreal in both
These ways so too is composition,
Because composition is unreal
So too in fact are forms.

361 Also because consciousnesses, feelings,
Discriminations and factors of composition each
Are not self-existent realities in any way,
[Pleasures] are not ultimately real.

362 Just as a lessening of pain
Is fancied to be real pleasure,
So a suppression of pleasure
Is also fancied to be pain.

363 Thus attachment to finding pleasure
And to separating from pain
Are to be abandoned because they do not inherently
Exist; thereby for those who see thus there is liberation.

364 What sees [reality]? Conventionally they say
It is the mind, for without mental factors
There can be no mind, and [a second mind],
Because unreal, cannot be simultaneous.[40]

365 Knowing thus truly and correctly
That animate beings are unreal,
Not being subject [to rebirth] and without grasping, one
Passes [from suffering] like a fire without its cause.

366 Bodhisattvas also who have seen it thus,
Seek perfect enlightenment with certainty,
They maintain a continuity of existence
Until enlightenment only through their compassion.

367 The collections [of merit and wisdom] of Bodhisattvas
    Were taught by the Tathāgata in the Mahāyāna,
    Disliked by the bewildered
    The Mahāyāna is derided.

368 Either through not knowing virtues and defects,
    Or identifying the defective as virtuous,
    Or through disliking virtues,
    They deride the Mahāyāna.

369 He who despises the Mahāyāna,
    Knowing that to harm others is wrong
    But that to help them is virtuous,
    Is called one who dislikes virtues.

370 He who despises Mahāyāna, the source
    Of all virtues in that [it teaches] taking delight
    Solely in the aims of others and not looking
    To one's own, consequently burns himself.

371 One with faith [in emptiness forsakes it] through mis-
        conception,
    Another who is angry [forsakes emptiness] through
        disliking it;
    If even the faithful one is said to be burned, what can be
        said
    About the one who is disinclined through despising it?

372 Just as it is explained in medicine
    That poison can be driven out by poison,
    What contradiction is there in saying that
    The injurious can be driven out by suffering?

373 It is widely known that motivation
Determines practices and that the mind
Is most important. How then could even suffering not be
   helpful
For one who gives assistance with the motivation to
   help others?

374 If even [in ordinary life] pain can bring future benefit,
[Accepting suffering] beneficial for
One's own and others' happiness of course will help;
This practice from of old is known as the excellent
   method.

375 Through relinquishing small pleasures
There is extensive happiness [later];
Seeing the greater happiness, the resolute
Should relinquish their small pleasures [now].

376 If such things cannot be borne,
Then doctors giving pungent
Medicines would disappear. It is not [reasonable]
To forsake [great pleasure for the small].

377 Sometimes what is normally thought unhelpful
Is regarded as beneficial by the wise;
General rules and their exceptions
Are highlighted in all treatises.

378 Who with intelligence would deride
Deeds motivated by compassion
And the stainless wisdom as explained
In the Mahāyāna?

379 Due to the great extent and depth
Of the Mahāyāna, it is derided
Through ignorance by the untrained and lazy,
Who are the foes of themselves and others.

380 The Mahāyāna has a nature
Of giving, ethics, patience, effort,
Concentration, wisdom and compassion,
How could it ever explain things badly?

381 Others' aims are [achieved] through giving and ethics,
One's own are [achieved] through patience and effort,
Concentration and wisdom cause liberation,
These epitomise the sense of the Mahāyāna.

382 The aims of benefiting oneself and others and the
        meaning
Of liberation as briefly taught [in the Hīnayāna]
By Buddha are contained in the six perfections,
Therefore the Mahāyāna is the word of Buddha.

383 Those blind with ignorance cannot bear
The Mahāyāna where Buddha taught
The great path of enlightenment
Consisting of merit and wisdom.

384 A Conqueror is said to have attributes that cannot be
        conceived because
The attributes [which are his causes] are inconceivable
        like the sky,
Therefore let the great nature of a Buddha as
Explained in the Mahāyāna be accepted.

385 Even [Buddha's] ethics were beyond
The scope of Śāriputra, so why
Is the inconceivable great nature
Of a Buddha not accepted?

386 The teaching in the Mahāyāna of non-production
And of extinction in the Hīnayāna are the same
Emptiness [since they show that inherent existence] is
    extinguished
And that nothing [inherently existent] is produced;
Then let the Mahāyāna be accepted [as Buddha's word].

387 If emptiness and the great nature
Of a Buddha are viewed thus with reason,
How could what is taught in the two vehicles
Be of unequal value for the wise?[41]

388 What the Tathāgata taught with a special
Intention is not easy to understand.
Because he taught one as well as three vehicles
You should therefore protect yourself through indiffer-
    ence.[42]

389 There is no fault with indifference, but there is fault
From despising it; how then could there be virtue?
Therefore those who seek good for themselves
Should not despise the Mahāyāna.

390 Since all the aspirations, deeds and
Dedications of Bodhisattvas
Were not explained in the Hearers' vehicle, how then
Could one become a Bodhisattva through its path?

391 [In the Vehicle of the Hearers] Buddha did not explain
The bases for a Bodhisattva's enlightenment;
What greater authority for this
Is there than the Conqueror?

392 How could the fruit of Buddhahood be superior
[If achieved] through the path common to Hearers
Which has the bases [of the Hearer enlightenment], the
     meanings of
The four noble truths and the auxiliary aids to en-
lightenment?

393 The subjects based on the deeds of Bodhisattvas
Were not mentioned in the [Hīnayāna] sūtras,
But were explained in the Mahāyāna, thus the clear
Sighted should accept it [as the word of Buddha].

394 Just as a grammarian [first] makes
His students read the alphabet,
So Buddha taught his trainees
The doctrines which they could bear.

395 To some he taught doctrines
To discourage sinning,
To some, doctrines for achieving merit,
To others, doctrines based on duality.

396 To some he taught doctrines based on non-duality, to
     some
He taught what is profound and frightening to the
     fearful,
Having an essence of emptiness and compassion,
The means of achieving [the highest] enlightenment.

397 Therefore the wise should extinguish
Any hatred for the Mahāyāna
And generate especial faith
To achieve perfect enlightenment.

398 Through faith in the Mahāyāna
And through the practices explained therein
The highest enlightenment is attained
And along the way all pleasures.

399 At that time [when you are a king] you should inter-
nalise
Firmly the practices of giving, ethics and patience,
Which were especially taught for householders
And which have an essence of compassion.

400 However, if through the unrighteousness
Of the world it is hard to rule religiously,
Then it is right for you to become a monk
For the practice and grandeur [to which it leads].

Chapter Five
The Bodhisattva Deeds

401 Having become a monk you should train
First with energy [in ethics],
Then take up the discipline of individual emancipation,
Hear [the scriptures recited] frequently, and ascertain their meaning.

402 Then, knowing the small faults, forsake
The sources to be forsaken;
With effort you should realise
Fully the fifty-seven faults.

403 Anger is a disturbance of mind,
Enmity disturbs it further,
Concealment is a hiding of faults,
Resentment a clinging to faulty ways.

404 Dishonesty is extreme deception,
Dissimulation, crookedness of mind,
Jealousy is to be hurt by the good qualities
Of others; miserliness is a fear of giving.

405 To be unembarrassed and unashamed
Is insensibility to oneself and others,
Inflatedness leads to disrespect,
While evil effort is a pollution from anger.

406   Arrogance is haughtiness,
Non-conscientiousness is to neglect
Virtues, pride has seven forms
Each of which I will explain.

407   Boasting that one is lower than the lowly,
Or equal with the equal, or greater than
Or equal to the lowly
Is called the pride of selfhood.

408   Boasting that one is equal to those
Who by some quality are better than oneself
Is the pride of being superior. Thinking
That one is higher than the extremely high,

409   Who fancy themselves to be superior,
Is pride greater than pride;
Like an abscess in a tumour
It is very vicious.

410   Conceiving an 'I' through ignorance
In the five empty [aggregates]
Which are called the appropriation
Is said to be the pride of thinking 'I'.

411   Thinking one has won fruits not yet
Attained is pride of conceit.
Praising oneself for faulty deeds
Is known by the wise as wrongful pride.

412   Deriding oneself, thinking
'I am senseless,' is called
The pride of lowliness.
Such briefly are the seven prides.

413 Hypocrisy is to control the senses
For the sake of goods and respect,
Flattery is to speak pleasant phrases
For the sake of goods and respect.

414 Indirect acquisition is to praise
The wealth of others so as to win it,
Artful acquisition is to deride
Others in order to acquire their goods.

415 Desiring to add profit to profit
Is to praise previous acquisitions,
Reciting faults is to repeat
The mistakes made by others.

416 Non-collectedness is selfish excitement
That is inconsiderate of others,
Clinging is the attachment of
The lazy to their bad possessions.

417 Making differences is discrimination
Obscured through desire, hatred or confusion,
Not looking into the mind is explained
As not applying it to anything.

418 One who through laziness loses respect and reverence
For those doing practices that are similar
Is a spiritual guide who follows not the ways
Of the Blessed One; he is regarded as bad.

419 Attachment is a small entanglement
Arising from desire,
When strong it is a great entanglement
Arising from desire.

420 Fondness is an attitude
Of clinging to one's own property,
Unsuitable fondness is attachment
To the property of others.

421 Irreligious lust is the libidinous praise
Of women who [in fact] are to be abandoned.
Hypocrisy is [to pretend] that one possesses
Good qualities which one lacks, while desiring sins.

422 Great desire is extreme greed gone beyond
The fortune of knowing satisfaction,
Desire for gain is wanting to be known
Always as having superior qualities.

423 Non-endurance is an inability to bear
Injury and suffering; impropriety
Is not to respect the activities
Of a spiritual guide or teacher.

424 Not heeding advice is not respecting
Counsel from those of similar practice.
Intention to meet with relatives
Is loving attachment to one's kindred.

425 Attachment to objects is to relate
Their qualities in order to acquire them.
Fancying immortality is to be
Unaffected by concern over death.

426 Intention endowed with making
[One's qualities] understood
Is the thought that due to the appearance of knowledge
And wealth others will take one as a guide.

427 Intention endowed with desire is a wish
     To help others motivated by desire.
     To be affected with harmful intent
     Implies that one wishes to harm others.

428 Dislike is a mind that is unsteady,
     Desiring union is a dirtied mind,
     Indifference is a body without
     Effort, a laziness of lassitude.

429 Being affected is the influence
     On body and colour by afflictions,
     Not wishing for food is explained
     As discomfort due to gorging.

430 A very weak mind is taught
     As timidity and fear,
     Longing for desires is to desire
     And seek after the five attributes.[43]

431 Harmful intent toward others arises
     From nine causes: having senseless qualms
     About oneself, one's friends and foes
     In the past, present and future.

432 Sluggishness is non-activity
     Due to a heavy mind and body,
     Sleep is slumber, excitement is a
     Lack of physical and mental peace.

433 Contrition is repentance for bad deeds
     Which arises afterwards from grief,
     Doubt is to be of two minds about
     The truths, the Three Jewels and so forth.

434   [Householder] Bodhisattvas abandon the above,
While those who keep a [monk's] vows strictly abandon
    more.
Freed from these defects
The virtues are easily observed.

435   Briefly the virtues observed
By Bodhisattvas are
Giving, ethics, patience, effort,
Concentration, wisdom, compassion and so forth.

436   Giving is to give away completely
All one's wealth, ethics is to help others,
Patience is to forsake anger,
Effort, to delight in virtues;

437   Concentration is unafflicted one-pointedness,
Wisdom is ascertainment of the meaning of the truths,
Compassion is a mind that savours only
Mercy and love for all sentient beings.

438   From giving there arises wealth, from ethics happiness,
From patience a good appearance, from [effort in]
    virtue
Brilliance, from concentration peace, from wisdom
Liberation, from compassion all aims are achieved.

439   From the simultaneous perfection
Of all those seven [virtues] is attained
The sphere of inconceivable wisdom
The protectorship of the world.

440 Just as the eight levels of Hearers
Are explained in their vehicle,
So are the ten Bodhisattva
Stages in the Mahāyāna.

441 The first of these is the Very Joyous
Since the Bodhisattva is rejoicing.
He forsakes the three entwinements[44] and is born
Into the lineage of the Tathāgatas.

442 Through the maturation of these qualities
The perfection of giving becomes supreme,
He vibrates a hundred worlds
And becomes a great lord of the world.

443 The second is called the Stainless
Because the ten [virtuous] actions
Of body, speech and mind are stainless
And he naturally abides in them.

444 Through the maturation of these qualities
The perfection of ethics becomes supreme,
He becomes a Universal Monarch helping beings,
Master of the glorious [four continents]
And of the seven precious substances.

445 The third stage is called the Shining because
The pacifying light of wisdom arises.
The concentrations and clairvoyances are generated,
While desire and hatred are extinguished completely.

446 Through the maturation of these qualities
He practises supremely the deeds of patience
And putting an end to desire completely
Becomes a great wise king of the gods.

447   The fourth is called the Radiant
      Because the light of true wisdom arises
      In which he cultivates supremely
      The auxiliaries of enlightenment.

448   Through the maturation of these qualities he becomes
      A king of the gods in [the heaven] Without Combat,[45]
      He is skilled in quelling the arising of the view
      That the transitory collection [is a real self].

449   The fifth is called the Extremely Difficult to Overcome
      Since all evil ones find it extremely hard to conquer
        him;
      He becomes skilled in knowing the subtle
      Meanings of the noble truths and so forth.

450   Through the maturation of these qualities he becomes
      A king of the gods abiding in the Joyous Heaven,[46]
      He overcomes the sources of afflictions
      And of the views of all Forders.

451   The sixth is called the Approaching because he is
      Approaching the qualities of a Buddha;
      Through familiarity with calm abiding and special
        insight
      He attains cessation and is thus advanced [in wisdom].

452   Through the maturation of these qualities he becomes
      A king of the gods [in the heaven] of Liking Emanation.[47]
      Hearers cannot surpass him, he pacifies
      Those with the pride of superiority.

453 The seventh is the Gone Afar because
   The number [of his qualities] has increased,
   Moment by moment he can enter
   The equipoise of cessation.

454 Through the maturation of these qualities he becomes a
      master
   Of the gods [in the heaven] of Control over Others'
      Emanations,[48]
   He becomes a great leader of teachers for he knows
   Direct realisation of the [four] noble truths.

455 The eighth is the Immovable, the youthful stage,
   Through non-conceptuality he is immovable
   And the spheres of his body, speech and mind's
   Activities are inconceivable.

456 Through the maturation of these qualities
   He becomes a Brahmā, master of a thousand worlds,
   Foe Destroyers and Solitary Realisers and so forth
   Cannot surpass him in establishing the meaning [of the
      doctrines].

457 The ninth stage is called
   Good Intelligence,
   Like a regent he has attained correct individual
   Realisation and therefore has good intelligence.

458 Through the maturation of these qualities
   He becomes a Brahmā who is master of a million worlds,
   Foe Destroyers and so forth cannot surpass him
   In responding to questions in the thoughts of sentient
      beings.

459   The tenth is the Cloud of Doctrine because
       The rain of excellent doctrine falls,
       The Bodhisattva is consecrated
       With light by the Buddhas.

460   Through the maturation of these qualities
       He becomes a master of the gods of Pure Abode,
       He is a supreme great lord, master
       Of the sphere of infinite wisdom.

461   Thus those ten stages are renowned
       As the ten of Bodhisattvas.
       The stage of Buddhahood is different,
       Being in all ways inconceivable,

462   Its boundless extent is merely said
       To encompass the ten powers;
       Each of his powers is immeasurable too
       Like [the limitless number] of all migrators.

463   The limitlessness of a Buddha's
       [Qualities] is said to be like
       That of space, earth, water, fire
       And wind in all directions.

464   If the causes are [reduced] to a mere
       [Measure] and not seen to be limitless,
       One will not believe the limitlessness
       [Of the qualities] of the Buddhas.

465   Therefore in the presence of an image
       Or reliquary or something else
       Say these twenty stanzas
       Three times every day:

466   Going for refuge with all forms of respect
      To the Buddhas, excellent Doctrine,
      Supreme Community and Bodhisattvas,
      I bow down to all that is worthy of honour.

467   From all sins I will turn away
      And thoroughly maintain all virtues,
      I will admire all the merits
      Of all embodied beings.

468   With bowed head and clasped hands
      I petition the perfect Buddhas
      To turn the wheel of doctrine and remain
      As long as beings transmigrate.

469   Through the merit of having done all this and through
      The merit that I have done and that I will do
      May all sentient beings aspire
      To the highest enlightenment.

470   May all sentient beings have all the stainless
      Powers, freedom from all conditions of non-leisure,
      Freedom of action
      And good livelihood.

471   May all embodied beings
      Have jewels in their hands and may
      All the limitless necessities of life remain
      Unconsumed as long as there is cyclic existence.

472   May all beings always be
      [Born] as superior humans,[49]
      May all embodied beings have
      Wisdom and the support [of ethics].

473 May embodied beings have a good complexion,
Good physique, great beauty, a pleasant appearance,
Freedom from disease,
Power and long life.

474 May all be skilled in the means [to extinguish
Suffering], and have liberation from it,
Absorption in the Three Jewels,
And the great wealth of Buddha's doctrine.

475 May they be adorned with love, compassion, joy,
Even-mindedness [devoid of] the afflictions,
Giving, ethics, patience, effort,
Concentration and wisdom.

476 May they have the brilliant major and minor marks [of a
Buddha]
From having finally completed the two collections [of
merit and wisdom]
And may they cross without interruption
The ten inconceivable stages.

477 May I also be adorned completely
With those and all other good qualities,
Be freed from all defects and possess
Superior love for all sentient beings.

478 May I perfect all the virtues
For which all embodied beings hope
And may I always relieve
The sufferings of all sentient beings.

479   May those beings in all worlds
       Who are distressed through fear
       Become entirely fearless
       Through merely hearing my name.

480   Through seeing or thinking of me
       Or only hearing my name may beings attain great joy,
       Naturalness free from error,
       Definiteness toward complete enlightenment,

481   And the five clairvoyances
       Throughout their continuum of lives.
       May I ever in all ways bring
       Help and happiness to all sentient beings.

482   May I always without harm
       Simultaneously stop
       All beings in all worlds
       Who wish to commit sins.

483   May I always be an object of enjoyment
       For all sentient beings according to their wish
       And without interference as are the earth,
       Water, fire, wind, medicine and forests.

484   May I be as dear to sentient beings as their
       Own life and may they be very dear to me,
       May their sins fructify for me
       And all my virtues for them.

485   As long as any sentient being
       Anywhere has not been liberated,
       May I remain [in the world] for his sake
       Even though I have attained enlightenment.

486   If the merit of this prayer
      Had form, it would never fit
      Into worlds as numerous
      As sand grains in the Ganges.

487   The Blessed One said so,
      And the reasoning is this:
      [The limitlessness of the merit of] wishing to help
        limitless realms
      Of sentient beings is like [the limitlessness of those
        beings].

488   These practices which I have
      Explained briefly to you
      Should always be as dear
      To you as your body.

489   He who feels a dearness for the practices
      Has in fact a dearness for his body;
      If dearness [for the body] helps it,
      The practices will do just that.

490   Therefore, pay heed to the practices as you do to your-
        self,
      Pay heed to achievement as you do to the practices,
      Pay heed to wisdom as you do to achievement,
      Pay heed to a wise man as you do to wisdom.

491   He who has qualms that [reliance] on one who has
      Purity, love, intelligence and helpful
      Appropriate speech would be bad for himself,
      Causes his own interests to be destroyed.

492　The qualifications of spiritual
　　　Guides should be known in brief by you;
　　　If you are taught by those who know
　　　Contentment, have compassion, ethics

493　And the wisdom which can drive out your afflictions,
　　　You should know [how to rely on] and respect them.
　　　You will attain the supreme achievement
　　　By following this excellent system:

494　Speak the truth, speak gently to sentient beings,
　　　Say what is by nature pleasant,
　　　What is [beneficial], most difficult to find;
　　　Speak to a plan, not defaming;
　　　Speak independently and well.

495　Be well-disciplined, contained, generous,
　　　Brilliantly attentive, of peaceful mind,
　　　Not excitable, nor deceitful,
　　　Not procrastinating, but steadfast.

496　Be certain like the moon [when it is] full
　　　And radiant like the sun in autumn,
　　　Be deep like the ocean
　　　And firm like Mount Meru.

497　Freed from all defects, adorned
　　　With all the virtues, become
　　　The sustenance of all sentient
　　　Beings and be omniscient.

498 These doctrines were not taught
Merely to help kings,
But with the wish in any way
To help other sentient beings.

499 O King, for you it would be right
Each day to think of this advice
So that you and others may achieve
Complete and perfect enlightenment.

500 For the sake of enlightenment the diligent should always
apply
Themselves to ethics, patience, non-jealousy and non-
miserliness;
Always respect a superior teacher and help
Altruistically without hope [of reward] those bereft of
wealth,
Always remain with superior people, leaving
The non-superior and maintaining thoroughly the
doctrine.

Here ends the *Precious Garland of Advice for the King* by the
great teacher, the Superior, Nāgārjuna. It was [first] translated by the Indian Abbot Vidyākāraprabhā and the Tibetan
translator monk Pel-tsek (dPal-brtsegs). Consulting three
Sanskrit editions, the Indian abbot Śikanakavarma and the
Tibetan monk Pa-tsap-nyi-ma-drak (Pa-tshab-nyi-ma-grags)
corrected mistranslations and other points which did not accord
with the particular thought of the Superior [Nāgārjuna] and
his 'son' [Āryadeva]. It was printed at the great publishing
house below [the Potala in Lhasa].

Guide to the Stanzas
by Gyel-tsap (rGyal-tshab)

Notes

1 The fruits previously described were effects within a human life which accord with the causes. Here, concordant effects as entire lifetimes in bad migrations are indicated.

2 'In fact' means 'ultimately' or 'as existing able to bear analysis'.

3 The surviving Sanskrit text is a little different here as in verses 47, 49, 51, 102, 123, 130, 138, 142, 342, etc. However, the Tibetan texts are followed because the translations into Tibetan were compared with three Sanskrit texts.

4 The production of suffering is caused by the conception of inherent existence, its cessation is caused by the path.

5 Previous to and simultaneously with their effects.

5a The Sanskrit has another interpretation which is offered by the other Tibetan edition: 'When there is no tall, / Short does not exist through its own nature, / Just as due to the non-production of a flame, / Light also does not arise.'

6 The followers of Kaṇāda, i.e., the Vaiśeṣikas.

7 Sanskrit for the last two lines: 'How could the produced, the stayed / And the ceased exist in fact?'

8 It is not seen that only a part of a thing changes. Also, if an atom changed completely, it could not be said, as the Vaiśeṣikas do, that it is permanent but its states are impermanent.

9 'Baseless' means not providing a base for the conception that things inherently exist.

10 'Forders' are, in Sanskrit, *Tīrthika*, i.e., non-Buddhists who propound and follow a path or ford to liberation or high status.

11 The aggregates and the self are not inexpressible as either one or different because all phenomena are either one or different.

12 Water, fire and wind; or cohesion, heat and motility.

13 The potencies of the four elements are said to be present in everything; the predominance of one element over the others determines what is manifested.

14 The constituents are earth, water, fire, wind, space and consciousness which are imputed to be a self.

15 See note 14.

16 It has already been established that there are no inherently existent things and no inherently existing trueness; thus, there are no inherently existent non-things or inherently existent falseness, because the latter exist only in relation to the former.

17 An objector wonders, 'Innumerable Buddhas are effecting the liberation of even more sentient beings; there are no new sentient beings; thus in time all would be liberated. Since of course such extinguishing or liberating of worldly beings does not increase the number of beings, the world must eventually have an end. Thus, why did Buddha remain silent about an end to the world?'

18 The first extreme of the world's having limits is propounded by the Nihilists who say that the self is finished in this life and does not go on to a future life. The second extreme of the world's not having limits is propounded by the Sāmkhyas who say that the self of this life goes to the next life. The third extreme of the world's both having and not having limits is propounded by the Jainas who say that the states of the self have limits but the nature of the self has no limits. The fourth extreme of the world's neither having nor not having limits is propounded by the Buddhist Proponents of a Self (Pudgalavādin) who say that there is a real self which is utterly unpredictable as permanent or impermanent.

19 Those who accept emptiness but take it to mean nothingness.

20 Those who take emptiness to mean a denial of cause and effect and therefore reject emptiness.

21 'Speaking pleasantly' is conversation based on high status and definite goodness. 'Behaving with purpose' is causing others to practise what is helpful. 'Concordance' is for one to practise what one teaches others.

22 Sometimes a horrible effect of a bad deed is seen in this life and sometimes it is not seen until the next life. If comfort is taken because the effects are not seen, why is fear of those actions not generated when the effects are seen?

23 The nine orifices are eyes, ears, nose, mouth, genitals and anus.

24 Reliquaries here are actual Buddhas.

24a This is a round, fleshy swelling on the crown or top of a Buddha's head; it is perceptible but its size is not.

25 A circle of hairs between the brows.

26 The chapter has an extra verse and Gyel-tsap (rGyal-tshab) does not comment on this verse which also has an extra line; therefore, it is set off in brackets.

27 This pain is a special form of virtue, and the word does not imply that it is unwanted.

28 The last line follows an alternative reading given by Gyel-tsap. Otherwise, it is, 'And respectfully rely on them with the six practices.'

29 Tīrthika.

30 Spells for relieving illness and the names and purposes of medicines are to be posted.

31 Sugar, ghee, honey, sesame oil and salt.

32 The skill of reducing many emanations to one and vice versa, etc.

33 Building temples and enduring difficulties for the sake of the doctrine.

34 The Tibetan translation offers two meanings for the last Sanskrit line, the first using *yasmāt* and the second *tasmāt*.

35 'Great exaltation' refers to the wide scope of his temple building and other public services.

36 Tibetan omits 'clothing'.

37 The objects apprehended by the other senses cannot be known to be pleasurable because the thought of pleasure can pay attention only to one object at a time.

38 The present must depend on the past and the future in order to be present, but if the present does not exist in the past and future, then it cannot truly depend on them. If the present does exist in the past and the future, then it is not different from them.

39 If the four elements were completely intermingled, they would lose their individual characters.

40 Is there a mind which certifies the existence of a mind cognising reality? If there were a second mind perceiving the first mind and existing simultaneously, it could certify the true existence of the first; however, all minds depend on mental factors and are thus unreal; also the certifier would need a certifier. Thus, only conventionally is it said that the mind sees reality.

41 The inequality would be to consider one as the word of Buddha and one as not.

42 If due to the complexity of Buddha's teaching one cannot understand it, indifference or neutrality is best.

43 Forms, sounds odours, tastes and tangible objects.

44 Viewing the mental and physical aggregates which are a transitory collection as a real self, afflicted doubt and considering bad ethics and disciplines to be superior.

45 Yāma.

46 Tuṣita.

47 Nirmāṇarati.

48 Paranirmitavaśavartin.

49 This is translated in accordance with Nāgārjuna's views as set forth in his works on the Highest Yoga Tantra (Anuttarayogatantra).

IV

The Song of the Four Mindfulnesses Causing the Rain of Achievements to Fall

Instructions for Meditation on the View of Emptiness

KAYSANG GYATSO
The Seventh Dalai Lama

With Commentary by
TENZIN GYATSO
The Fourteenth Dalai Lama

Edited and translated by
Jeffrey Hopkins
and Lati Rimpoche

Introduction

The fourth work in this volume is a short poem that contains within it the essentials of sūtra and tantra:

1 The admiration for one who teaches the path to enlightenment.
2 The thought definitely to leave cyclic existence and the consequent wish to attain highest enlightenment in order to help all sentient beings.
3 The simultaneous and swift collection of merit and wisdom through imagining oneself as a deity who is qualified by emptiness.
4 The realisation of emptiness which is coupled with its application to the world of appearances.

For the sake of easy memorisation and subsequent application in meditation the Seventh Dalai Lama (1708–57) versified these concise teachings, which were originally given by Mañjuśrī to Tsong-ka-pa. The translation is based on oral transmissions and explanations of the text received from His Holiness Tenzin Gyatso, the Fourteenth Dalai Lama, in Dharamsala, India, in May and August of 1972. These explanations were recorded, translated, and edited and constitute the prose commentary surrounding the verses.

Jeffrey Hopkins

Instructions for Meditation on the View of Emptiness, The Song of the Four Mindfulnesses, Causing the Rain of Achievements to Fall

Initially, one observes the suffering of cyclic existence, goes for refuge, and performs guru yoga, visualising the sources of refuge and petitioning them to remain in the world and teach the doctrine; this is the mindfulness of the guru. Then, one observes other sentient beings' suffering in cyclic existence and, due to their dearness to oneself, generates love and compassion which thereupon induce an altruistic mind of enlightenment—the wish to attain Buddhahood for the sake of others—the second mindfulness. Due to this, the divine guru enters oneself, transforming one's own body, speech, and mind into that of a deity, the third mindfulness. Then, the actual session of practice is constituted by meditation on the view of emptiness, the fourth mindfulness, in which a union of calm abiding and special insight is cultivated in conjunction with tantra.

Kaysang Gyatso set these four practices into five stanzas for the sake of ease in memorisation and, thereby, adaptability for practice. The first stanza is concerned with how to rely on a spiritual guide:

1 *Mindfulness of the Guru*

On the seat of the immutable union of method and wisdom
Sits the kind guru who is the entity of all the refuges,
A Buddha who has perfect abandonment and wisdom is there.
Forsaking thoughts of defects, make a petition with pure perception,
Not letting your mind stray, place it within admiration and respect,
Making your attention unforgetful, maintain it within admiration and
  respect.

Because the guru possesses a union of method and wisdom—compassion and realisation of emptiness—he is said to abide on the seat of the immutable union of method and wisdom. In another way that accords with Highest Yoga Tantra, the seat is in one's own heart and is comprised of the red and white drops, indestructible until enlightenment and thus immutable, and on this seat is one's kind guru. The practice of considering the guru to be present in one's own heart is conducive to conceiving one's body, speech, and mind as undifferentiable from the guru's.

He is the guru, personal deity, sky-goer, Buddha, and Bodhisattva—the essence of all sources of refuge. Though the great masters of the past, such as Nāgārjuna, were indeed very kind to write such great texts, they are now only objects of memory and even if we thought, 'How nice it would be to meet Nāgārjuna', we could not. At this point in our spiritual development we are like sick persons unable to move about even with a cane; we are like the very young or the very old, unable to sustain ourselves, and since in this dire situation the guru is the sustainer, he is viewed as the essence of all sources of refuge.

The kind guru should always be considered as abiding in one's heart; thus, the Buddha who has abandoned all obstructions and attained complete realisation is not to be sought externally but identified in the centre of the heart. This is the ultimate guru, the innate wisdom of the mode of subsistence of all phenomena.

Since the guru is a fully qualified Buddha, one should forsake the conception that he has defects, such as ordinary activities. Within mindfulness and awareness one should train in admiration and respect.

2   *Mindfulness of the Altruistic Aspiration to Highest Enlightenment*

In the prison of the suffering of limitless cyclic existence
Wander the six types of sentient beings[1] bereft of happiness,
Fathers and mothers who protected you with kindness are there.
Forsaking desire and hatred, cultivate endearment and compassion,
Not letting your mind stray, place it within compassion,
Making your attention unforgetful, maintain it within compassion.

Sentient beings want happiness but are bereft of happiness; they do not want suffering but are continuously tortured with suffering. The place where the six types of beings wander is cyclic existence, the limitless forms of which are prisons, created by the power of contaminated actions and afflictions. These suffering beings are not unrelated to oneself; rather, because they have extended continuous kindness over one's beginningless continuum of lives, one has responsibility for them.

These persons, wandering in cyclic existence, are not to be differentiated into groups with some desired and others hatred; all are to be helped. Forsaking desire and hatred, one should cherish them more than oneself, continuously generating the compassionate wish that they might be freed from suffering and the causes of suffering.

The description of the condition of cyclic existence implies the need to generate an intention definitely to leave this state of suffering, but the thrust of the second mindfulness is to generate compassion for others since it is the root of the altruistic mind of enlightenment. If such a good mind does not arise, then one is bereft of the very basis of the Mahāyāna.

How can one relieve these sentient beings from suffering and the causes of suffering? One can provide vast benefit only by achieving Buddhahood and working for their welfare within that state; therefore, one must do whatever is possible to attain Buddhahood.

3   *Mindfulness of Your Body as a Divine Body*

When this altruistic attitude, the wish to attain Buddhahood for the sake of others, is so strong that one cannot bear delay in accomplishing others' welfare even for an hour, one views the present ineffectual situation as a waste of valuable time. What is the method for quickly attaining Buddhahood? By means of training in Mantra and particularly in the wisdom of non-dual bliss and emptiness, one can achieve Buddhahood in a single lifetime. In this practice a subtle mind realising emptiness is generated as a blissful entity,

and to develop this special meditative stabilisation of bliss and emptiness, the base of the bliss—one's own body—must be visualised as a
divine body. This involves stopping both the appearance and conception of ordinariness.

In the divine mansion of great bliss, pleasant to feel,
Abides the divine body which is your own body of pure aggregates and
   constituents,[2]
A deity with the Three Bodies[3] *inseparable is there.*
Not conceiving yourself to be ordinary, practise divine pride and vivid
   appearance,
Not letting your mind stray, place it within the profound and the
   manifest,[4]
Making your attention unforgetful, maintain it within the profound and
   the manifest.

Whatever appears is seen as empty; whatever is empty is experienced
as bliss; and whatever is blissful appears as the sport of a deity.
When this is realised, the objects of the six senses act as aids in
generating bliss and thus are 'pleasant to feel'.

Everything appears as endless purity. When an environment
appears, it is the sport of bliss, and when a being appears, that person
is also the sport of bliss. One's own impure mental and physical
aggregates and constituents shine as the sport of a deity; thus, a
divine body is not to be identified externally but is one's own body
viewed as a divine entity.

Since one believingly practises the generation of oneself as one's
own personal deity and trains in this vivid appearance and divine
pride until they become firm, the Three Buddha Bodies—Truth
Body, Enjoyment Body, and Emanation Body—are present.
For instance, when cultivating the stage of generation in Highest
Yoga Tantra, the Three Bodies are gradually manifested, and since
one is then undifferentiable from a deity, the pride thinking,
'I am the deity,' arises. Due to this divine pride, one does not conceive of oneself as ordinary but sustains a firm sense of divinity

within clear appearance, maintaining one's mind in the profound—observing emptiness—and in the manifest—observing the divine body.

4 *Mindfulness in the View of Emptiness*

Since this poem is mainly concerned with instructions on the view of emptiness, it has two stanzas on this topic, one each for the mode of sustaining the space-like meditative equipoise and for the mode of sustaining the illusion-like subsequent realisation.

Throughout the circle of appearing and occurring objects of knowledge
Pervades the space of clear light, the nature of phenomena, the ultimate,
An inexpressible mode of being of objects is there.
Forsaking mental fabrications,[5] *look to the entity of immaculate emptiness,*
Not letting your mind stray, place it within the nature of phenomena,
Making your attention unforgetful, maintain it within the nature of phenomena.

At the cross-roads of the varieties of appearances and the six consciousnesses
Is seen the confusion of the baseless phenomena of duality,
The illusory spectacles of a deceiving magician are there.
Not thinking they are true, look to their entity of emptiness,
Not letting your mind stray, place it within appearance and emptiness,
Making your attention unforgetful, maintain it within appearance and emptiness.

All phenomena are established in the sphere of emptiness of inherent existence, devoid of their own inner principle. Thus, although the circle of appearing and occurring objects of knowledge is boundless and limitless, they are all of one taste in the sphere of the nature of phenomena; there is no object not pervaded by this empty nature.

Just as the circle of objects of knowledge pervades space, so the objective clear light, the ultimate truth, pervades all objects of knowledge; it is their mode of being. It is not newly fabricated or created by the mind; from the very inception of any phenomenon its emptiness of inherent existence abides as its nature. This status of objects cannot be expressed with words or experienced in thought by ordinary beings in the way that Superiors perceive it; beyond terms and thoughts, it is inexpressible.

There is no need to search for the mode of being of objects elsewhere; it is right with these objects. As Aryadeva's *Four Hundred (Catuḥśataka)* says, 'All these are empty of inherent existence,' using the term of proximity, 'these'. Since the ultimate truth exists as the nature of all appearances, if one analyses, the mode of being is right here.

Though it is said in scripture that all phenomena are merely imputedly existent, one must first analyse whether phenomena appear as if they only imputedly exist or not. They certainly do not; they appear to exist objectively. If they did exist in the concrete way that they seem to possess, they would have to be findable when sought analytically. However, when one trains in accordance with the modes of analysis taught in Nāgārjuna's *Fundamental Treatise on the Middle Way (Mūlamadhyamakaśāstra)* one gradually comes to a decision that although phenomena appear to be self-established, they do not at all exist that way. Then, deep vivid ascertainment that merely eliminates inherent existence is induced in the sense that no objective existence can be posited in the face of this ascertainment. When the mere vacuity that is a negative of inherent existence is experienced, one should fix on it one-pointedly; this is the mode of sustaining the space-like meditative equipoise.

Then, when one loosens the mode of observation of emptiness, the objects qualified by this empty nature appear as if pointable, 'This is such and such.' These various appearances—pure Buddhas, impure sentient beings, habitations, inhabitants, earth, water, fire, wind—shine forth as the objects of the six senses—eye, ear, nose, tongue, body, and mental consciousnesses. However, when one analyses whether these various appearances have their own self-established entity, it cannot be found. All things to be seen, heard, smelled, tasted, and touched are baseless, without their own inner nature, unstable, lacking their own independent capacity or subsistence, their own inner basis. Yet, whereas they are baseless, they falsely appear to have their own mode of subsistence. The obscured who adhere to these objects as existing the way they appear are deceived, like persons who believe that a magician's illusions are real.

Previously in meditative equipoise, non-inherent existence became clear to the mind, but now, subsequent to meditative equipoise, phenomena appear to exist in their own right whereas they do not. The illusion-like subsequent realisation is the composite of the appearance of objects as if inherently existent within knowledge that they are empty of inherent existence.

One must again and again view the empty nature of objects and then within this realisation practise the union of appearance and emptiness, in the context of which one can gain great ascertainment of dependent-arising. Through this, one's understanding that all phenomena are merely designated by terms and thoughts increases, and through that, the ascertainment that phenomena do not exist in their own right becomes more powerful. Again, through its force, subsequent to meditative equipoise the ascertainment that whatever appears is the sport of emptiness becomes more powerful.

With the two realisations helping each other in this way, one advances over the four levels of the path of preparation: heat, peak, forbearance, and supreme mundane qualities. With the opening and heightening of the appearance of the suchness of phenomena, one's realisation becomes even more profound, whereupon the truth is directly realised.

These instructions on the view of emptiness for one who uses the four mindfulnesses, special instructions actually bestowed by the holy Mañjughoṣa on Tsong-ka-pa, a king of doctrine, were composed by the Buddhist monk Losang Kaysang Gyatso (bLo-bzang-bskal-bzang-rgya-mtsho) for the sake of his own and others' establishing predispositions for the correct view.

Notes

1 Gods, demigods, humans, animals, hungry ghosts, and denizens of hells.

2 Earth or hardness, water or cohesiveness, fire or temperature, wind or currents, space or passageways, and consciousness.

3 Body of Truth or wisdom consciousness, Body of Enjoyment or spontaneous speech, and Body of Form or physical body.

4 Profound emptiness and manifest appearance.

5 Mental fabrications which posit an object negated by emptiness other than inherent existence.